MAKE AND CLOTHE
Your Own
DOLLHOUSE DOLLS

ELLEN BEDINGTON

MAKE AND CLOTHE
Your Own
DOLLHOUSE DOLLS

ELLEN BEDINGTON

CHARTWELL
BOOKS, INC.

A QUINTET BOOK

Published by Chartwell Books
A Division of Book Sales, Inc.
110 Enterprise Avenue
Secaucus, New Jersey 07094

This edition produced for sale in the U.S.A.,
its territories and dependencies only.

ISBN 1-55521-920-9

This book was designed and produced by
Quintet Publishing Limited
6 Blundell Street
London N7 9BH

Creative Director: Richard Dewing
Senior Editor: Laura Sandelson
Designer: James Lawrence
Editor: Lydia Darbyshire
Photographer: Jeremy Thomas

Typeset in Great Britain by
Central Southern Typesetters, Eastbourne
Manufactured in Singapore by
Eray Scan (Pte) Ltd
Printed in Singapore by
Star Standard Industries (Pte) Ltd

ACKNOWLEDGEMENT

The publishers would like to extend special
thanks to Lionel Barnard of *The Mulberry
Bush*, Brighton, Sussex, and Dijon Ltd,
Heathfield, Sussex for the loan of the doll's
house furniture used in the photographs.

CONTENTS

~

INTRODUCTION 7

~

MAKING THE DOLLS 9

~

DRESSING THE DOLLS 39

~

INTRODUCTION

*M*iniatures depicting the human form have been found in many places and countries for centuries, and doll-making and doll-dressing have a long history. Some of the most delightful of all dolls to make and dress are the miniatures – dolls that are 6 inches high or less, that can be dressed to make complete families to fill dollhouses.

A dollhouse doll can be dressed in any type of fabric, the decoration can be as simple or elaborate as you wish, and the dolls can be added to most collections without any fear of overcrowding. As space is often at a premium in today's smaller houses, more and more people are turning to collecting and making tiny dolls. It is an ideal way of escaping into a perfect make-believe world.

This book is designed to encourage and help you to enjoy making and dressing dollhouse dolls. Each step in the assembly and making of kits and the dolls' clothes has been illustrated and clearly explained. Some short cuts are included, and there are also some do's and don'ts, garnered from many years spent teaching this enthralling subject. You will find that many of the tools and equipment you need are ordinary household items, which helps to keep this pastime within the reach of most pockets.

To enjoy the hobby of making and dressing dolls, it is important to choose your own style of doll and keep to it. The last 10 years have seen a tremendous growth in the types of dolls and costumes that are available, and even the vast range of commercially produced models available can hardly keep up with the demand for new dolls and styles of clothes.

The dolls described and dressed in this book are "artist" dolls – that is, they are dolls designed and completed by an individual. These artist's dolls differ from reproduction dolls, which are copies of antique or modern dolls and which can be purchased in kit form or made from commercial molds. Two of the dolls described in this book have been made up from commercial kits, and two from molds – all of them, however, have been individually dressed and wigged.

If you have a passion for detail and enjoy working with precise measurements you will find this a satisfying hobby. It also incorporates several different craft skills, which makes it additionally challenging and rewarding. It also offers the opportunity, through modeling, for you to make some unique and wholly individual dolls, but even if you do not feel sufficiently skilful (or confident) or have no wish to model with clay, you can, through the use of kits, add your own character and personality to a doll with ready-made face, arms and legs.

The dolls made and dressed in this book will suit most modern dollhouses and many antique ones. They are made to the 1:12 scale, which is the standard size.

No two makers will approach the making of dollhouse dolls in exactly the same way. The instructions that follow have been designed to be as clear and straightforward as possible. However, never be afraid to change a technique or to try out something new. Put your own personality into each doll you make and remember always to make the dolls for yourself first and for other people second.

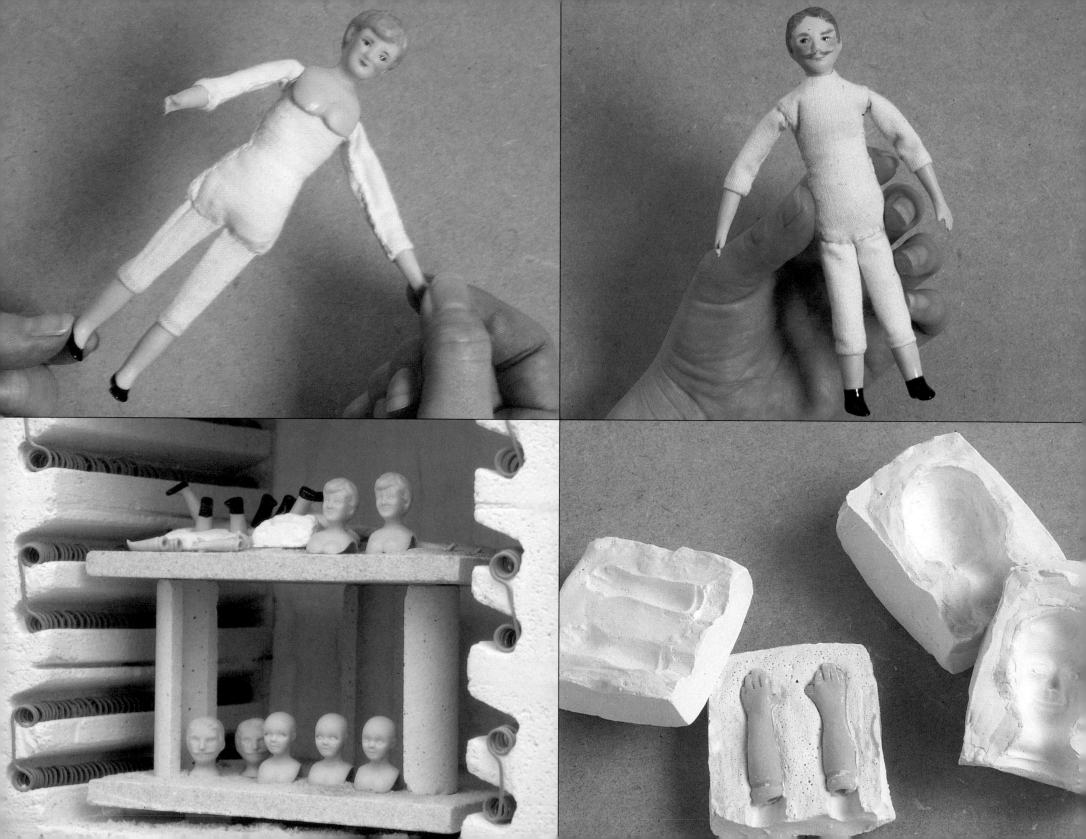

MAKING
DOLLHOUSE
DOLLS

*D*oll-making has improved beyond all recognition in recent years. There is now a wonderful range of materials and paints, both acrylic and oil, and doll-making kits and supplies of all kinds are widely and easily available.

You have only to open one of the many craft magazines that are now published to see an array of advertisements for kilns and molds and other doll-making paraphernalia. However, kilns and molds are expensive, and before you make such a major outlay, you should, perhaps, experiment with modeling clay to see if you want to take this aspect of the hobby further. Only if you plan to make large numbers of molded dolls (or, of course, if you intend to use the kiln for other purposes) will the expenditure be worthwhile. You may, in fact, want to consider attending one of the doll-making courses that are advertised in the craft magazines so that you can see all the stages involved before you decide to make such a large purchase.

The four dolls described in this section are of two kinds. The first two dolls are made from kits; one has a shoulder-plate, the other has a flange neck. The other two dolls are molded, one from a commercially supplied mold, the other from an individually made mold.

1

A SHOULDER-PLATE DOLL

~

THE DOLL MADE FROM THIS KIT HAS A HEAD
WITH AN INTEGRAL SHOULDER-PLATE AND IS
COMPLETE WITH MOLDED HAIR. USING A DOLL
WITH MOLDED HAIR ELIMINATES THE NEED TO
MAKE A WIG, AND ALMOST ALL ANTIQUE DOLL'S
HOUSE DOLLS ARE OF THIS TYPE. HOWEVER, YOU
CAN ADD A WIG IF YOU WISH. THE BODY FOR THIS
FIRST KIT IS ADAPTED FROM AN ORIGINAL
ANTIQUE BODY. BECAUSE ALL THAT IS REQUIRED
IS TO ATTACH THE ARMS AND LEGS TO A SIMPLE,
TWO-PIECE BODY, IT IS ONE OF THE EASIEST
DOLLS TO UNDERSTAND AND TO PUT TOGETHER.

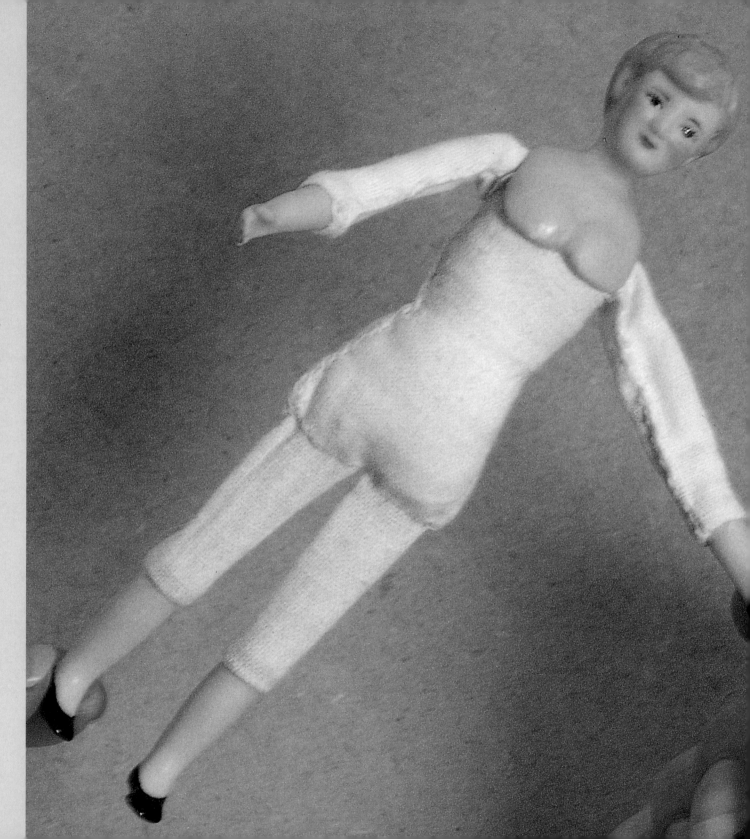

YOU WILL NEED

- Kit: painted porcelain head, lower arms and hands and lower legs and feet or shoes; the kit will usually also include the pattern for the body and pipe cleaners (6 for an adult doll, 3 for a child doll)
- Clear adhesive
- Scissors
- Tracing paper
- Pen or pencil
- 9 inch unbleached calico
- Needle, pins and sewing thread
- Small amount of soft white polyester stuffing
- Tweezers or small forceps

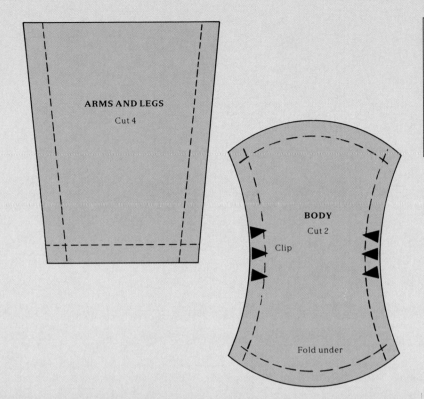

ARMS AND LEGS
Cut 4

BODY
Cut 2

Clip

Fold under

~ KITS ~

To enable you to make the shoulder-plate and flange-neck dolls to the correct size, actual size line diagrams have been included. As you make the dolls, lay the armature over the diagram to check that the finished doll will be the right height and have the correct proportions.

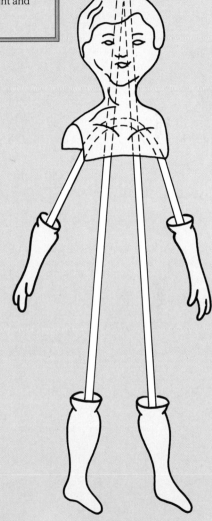

A shoulder-head doll. Note that the length of the arms from fingertip to fingertip should equal the height of the body. The wires for the leg armature pass through the shoulder-plate to the top of the head. A lady doll should be about 5¼ inches high.

1 | Glue the pipe cleaners into the legs.

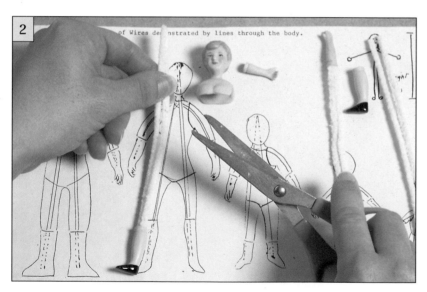

2 | Lay the leg and leg armatures on top of the pattern and cut each pipe cleaner so that it reaches the top of the head. Most shoulder-plate heads have an opening through the shoulder-plate through which the armature wires can pass.

3 | Glue one end of the pipe cleaners into one of the lower arm pieces and measure it against the pattern before cutting it to length. Glue the other arm piece in position. As a guide, the length of the arms from fingertip to fingertip should equal the height of the body.

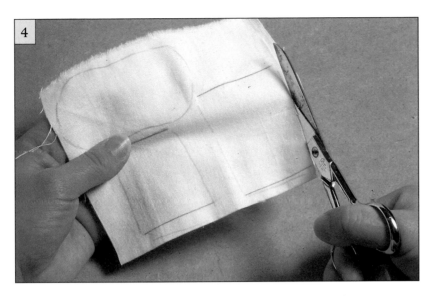

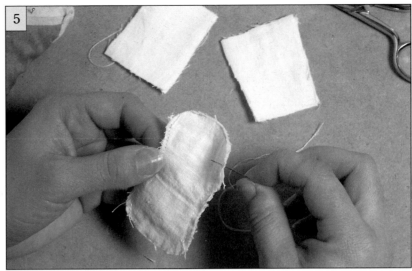

4 Trace around the templates for the body and the arms and legs and cut out two body pieces and four pieces for the arms and legs from the unbleached calico.

5 Leaving a seam allowance of ¼ inch, neatly stitch the two sides of the body together, leaving the top and bottom open. Clip the waist as indicated and turn to the right side.

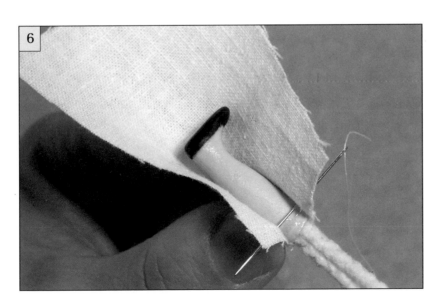

6 Make a pencil mark on the lower leg straight up from the heel to indicate where the seam will be. Put some adhesive in the groove around the top of the lower leg, place the leg on one of the cut-out leg pieces so that the fabric covers the leg, and carefully push the fabric into the groove with your thumbnail. Stitch together the part of the leg seam that is nearest to the porcelain lower leg and wind the thread around the groove three times to hold the fabric securely to the lower leg, opening out the seam allowance so that the fabric lies flat in the groove. Add a spot of adhesive to hold the thread in position. Repeat for other leg.

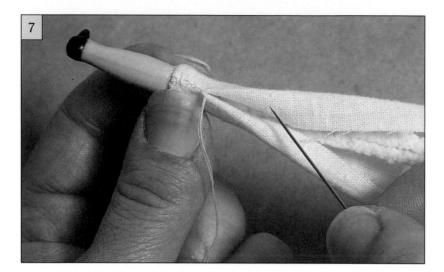

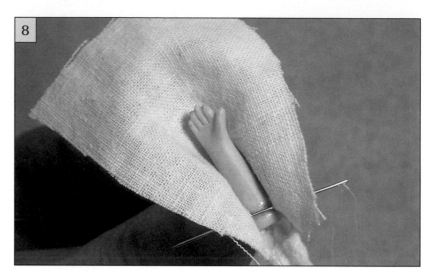

7 When the adhesive is dry, pull the fabric to cover the leg armature and neatly over-sew the seam, which should run up the back of the leg in line with the heel. Stuff the leg lightly and glue the top of the fabric to the leg armature, making sure that the fabric is smooth. Repeat for the other leg.

8 Attach the fabric pieces to the lower arms in the same way, but making a pencil mark on the inside – that is, the palm side – of the arm so that you can position the seam line to run under the arms. The arms will be attached to the leg armature at the top of the shoulder-plate. Check the position of the arms on the plan. Also make sure that the arms are the same length and that when they are slightly bent the fingertips are just below the level of the hips. Place the shoulder-plate over the arms and leg armatures to double check the length and position of the arms. When you are satisfied, glue the tops of the arms to the tops of the legs.

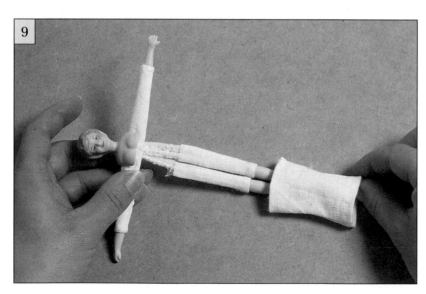

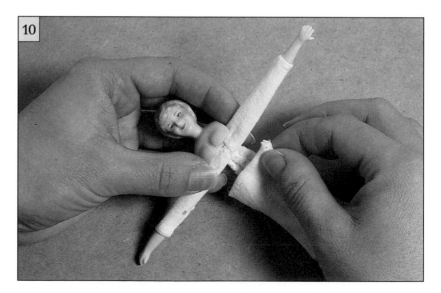

9 Push the body over the leg armatures up to the arms, checking the position against the plan.

10 With the shoulder-plate over the arms, hold the body in position at the shoulders with one or two stitches.

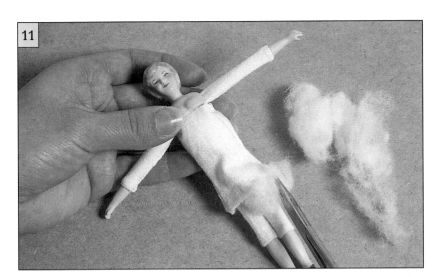

11 Use tweezers or small forceps to insert a small amount of polyester stuffing into the body, pushing it smoothly into the body around the front and back. Close the lower end of the body seam, turning in the seam allowance of ¼ inch and sewing across the legs.

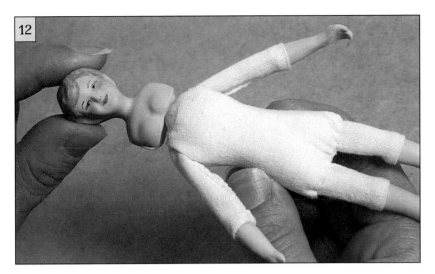

12 Check again that the shoulder-plate will fit snugly over the shoulders and top of the body. If the shoulder-plate will not fit or if the body is longer than indicated on the plan, remove a small amount of stuffing and increase the size of the seam allowance at the top of the body. Oversew the top seam of the body. When you are satisfied, glue the shoulder-plate into position, pushing it well down over body.

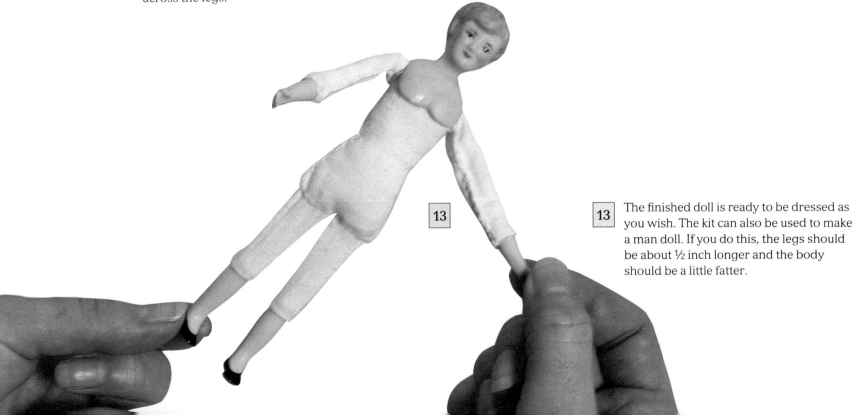

13 The finished doll is ready to be dressed as you wish. The kit can also be used to make a man doll. If you do this, the legs should be about ½ inch longer and the body should be a little fatter.

~ MAKING A MOHAIR WIG ~

The doll in the kit has molded and painted hair. If you want to dress her as a Victorian lady or if a doll does not have molded hair, you can either buy a ready-made wig with ringlets or make one yourself.

YOU WILL NEED

- Mohair or wool crepe for hair
- Plastic film
- Rubber band
- Clear adhesive
- Sewing thread to match mohair
- Hair setting lotion
- ⅛ inch knitting needle
- Scissors
- Tweezers or forceps

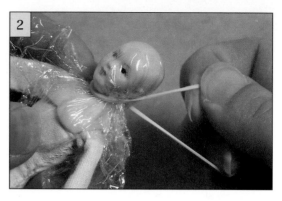

1 Gently brush the mohair, holding it down with one hand. Keep any loose hairs to one side.

2 Cover the doll's head with a small piece of plastic film, holding it in position with a rubber band around the doll's neck.

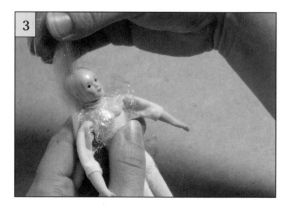

3 Put a thin layer of adhesive over the hair area of the plastic film, taking care to keep it within what will be the doll's hairline. Put some hair on the adhesive, placing it on the top of the head and taking it up and around the head to the back. Repeat the process if necessary.

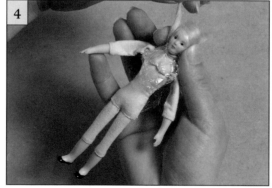

4 Twist the hair on top of the head and hold it in position with some matching sewing thread.

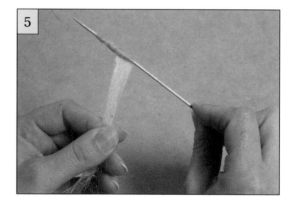

5 Take the loose pieces of mohair, dampen them with a little setting lotion and wind them tightly around a ⅛ inch knitting needle. Leave to dry, slip off the knitting needle and cut into ½ inch lengths to make ringlets. You will need eight ringlets in all.

6 Put spots of adhesive on the side of the wig and use tweezers or forceps to position the ringlets, so that there are four symmetrical ringlets at each side.

7 Remove the rubber band and peel off the plastic film with the mohair attached. Cut off the spare plastic film.

8 Trim the plastic film neatly to the hairline. Cover the head with a thin layer of adhesive and place the wig on the head, folding any visible pieces of plastic film neatly under the wig.

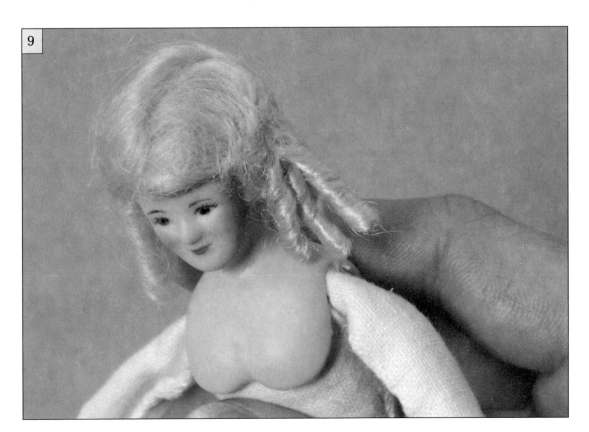

9 The finished wig.

2

A FLANGE-NECK DOLL

~

THIS FLANGE-NECK DOLLHOUSE DOLL CAN BE
MADE FROM ONE OF THE KITS THAT ARE
AVAILABLE FROM SOME CRAFT SHOPS. THE BODY
WAS DESIGNED SPECIALLY TO ALLOW THE HEAD
TO ROTATE, AND ALTHOUGH IT IS A LITTLE MORE
COMPLICATED THAN THE SHOULDER-PLATE
DOLL, IT IS WELL WORTH THE EFFORT.

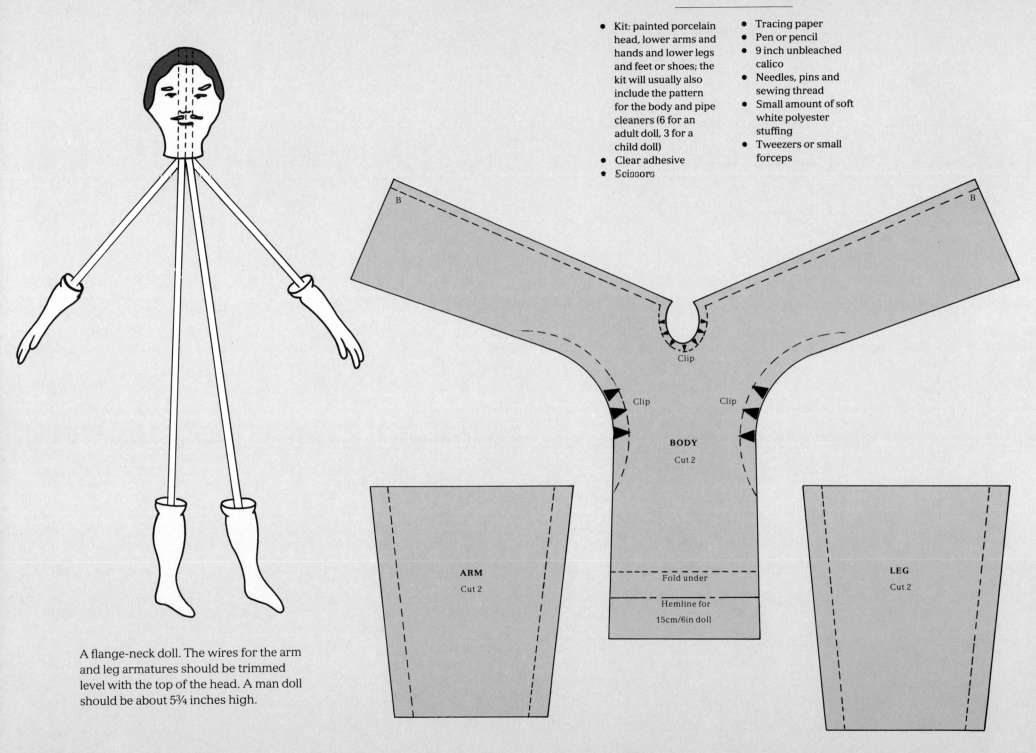

B

B

Clip

Clip

Clip

BODY

Cut 2

ARM

Cut 2

LEG

Cut 2

Fold under

Hemline for

15cm/6in doll

A flange-neck doll. The wires for the arm and leg armatures should be trimmed level with the top of the head. A man doll should be about 5¾ inches high.

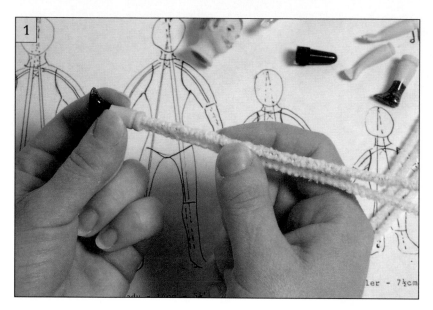

1 Glue pipe cleaners into the lower legs.

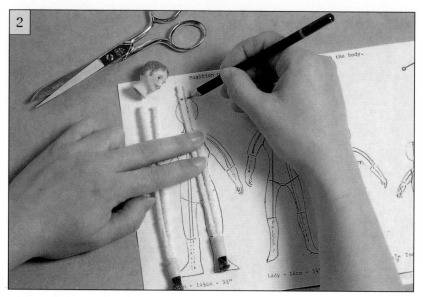

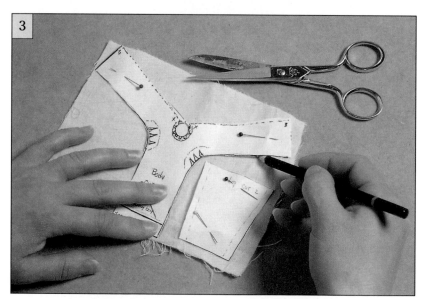

2 Place the head on the top end of the leg armatures and lay them on the pattern to check the length, marking the leg armatures at a point just below the bottom edge of the neck flange. Remove the head and mark on the leg armatures the top of the head, trimming them to this length. Glue pipe cleaners to one lower arm, measure it against the plan and glue the other lower arm in place. As a guide, the length of the arm from fingertip to fingertip should equal the overall height of the body.

3 Trace the templates for the body, arms and legs. Cut out two body pieces (one is a lining) and two each of the arm and leg pieces. Place the body pieces together, and stitch up one side of the back seam, around the neck edge and down the other back seam. Clip the neck curve to the stitching line and turn right side out. Press lightly.

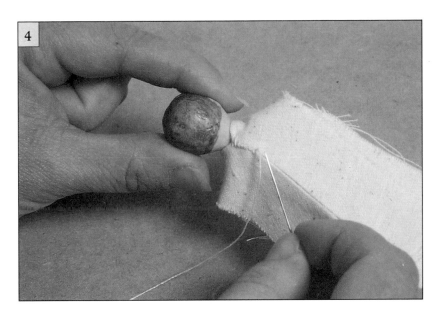

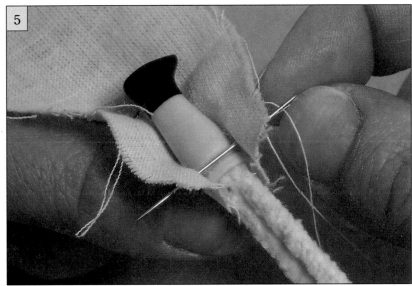

4 Stitch the neck around the flange of the neck, pulling it tight so that the neck will turn but will not fall out, then neatly oversew the back seam.

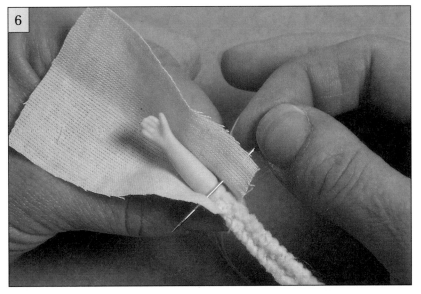

5 Mark a point on the legs with a pencil dot in line with the heel. Run some adhesive in the groove at the top of the leg and fold the fabric around the leg, using a thumbnail to push the fabric into the groove. Make sure that the seam is in line with the mark. Stitch through the seam and turn the fabric back. Wind the thread around the groove three times, fasten it off at the seam edge and finish it off with a dot of adhesive. Leave the adhesive to dry. Pull the fabric up over the leg armatures and oversew the leg seam neatly. Lightly stuff the leg, then pull the fabric up smoothly and glue it to the armature. Repeat for the other leg.

6 Mark the porcelain arm in line with the palm to indicate the position of the underarm seam. Run some adhesive into the groove in the arm and use your thumbnail to push the arm piece fabric into the groove, making sure that the seam remains in line with the dot. Stitch through the seam and turn the seam allowance back. Wind the thread around the groove three times, fasten it off at the seam edge and finish it off with a spot of adhesive. When the adhesive is dry, pull the fabric up over the arm and oversew the underarm neatly. Stuff the arm lightly and glue the fabric to the arm pipe cleaners, making sure that it is perfectly smooth. Repeat for the other arm.

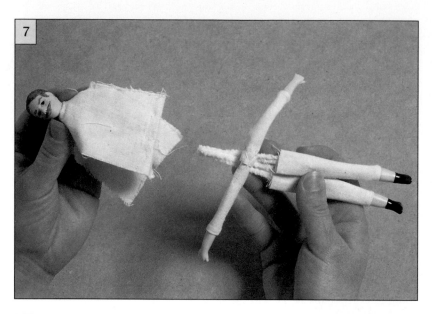

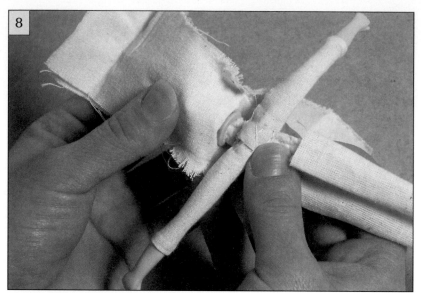

7 Glue the arms to the leg armature at the point marked for the bottom of the neck flange. Do not glue the neck flange, or the head will not move. Place the body with the head attached on the leg armature. The rim of the neck flange should rest on the wire of the arms.

8 Pull the body and head over the leg armature, pulling the body firmly down over the legs and pinning it in position. Make sure that the head is straight. Clip and turn under the shoulders, stitching them neatly to the arms. Use tweezers or small forceps to insert a little padding into the body, smoothing it evenly around front and back. Stitch the bottom seam over the legs, turning under the bottom seam allowance.

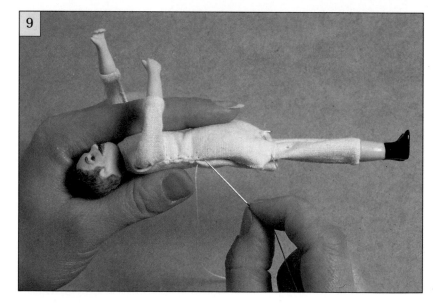

9 Pin the sides together, checking again that the head is straight. Add or take out stuffing if necessary, then carefully oversew the side seams. It will be easier to make sure that the head and body remain straight if you thread needles and sew down alternate sides for a short distance. Pull in the waist if you want a slimmer doll.

10 The finished man doll is now ready to be dressed in whatever way you wish.

3

USING A MOLD

~

SEVERAL STYLES OF MOLD ARE AVAILABLE FOR
MAKING DOLLS, BUT WE HAVE CHOSEN ANOTHER
SHOULDER-PLATE DOLL. USING A MOLD OFFERS
OPPORTUNITIES TO ALTER THE FACIAL DETAILS
AND THE HANDS, AND IT IS, THEREFORE, ONE OF
THE BEST WAYS OF MAKING A DOLL THAT IS
INDIVIDUAL AND, PERHAPS, PERFORMING A
SPECIFIC TASK.

THE HEAD OF THIS SHOULDER-PLATE DOLL IS
BALD, BUT YOU CAN MAKE A WIG AS DESCRIBED
ON PAGE 16.

AFTER A KILN, THE MOLDS ARE THE MOST
EXPENSIVE ITEMS NEEDED BY A DOLL-MAKER.
THEY ARE MADE FROM SUPERFINE PLASTER OF
PARIS, WHICH ABSORBS THE WATER FROM THE
CLAY, AND THEY ARE AVAILABLE FROM SOME
DOLLS SHOPS AND FROM HOBBY CERAMIC
SUPPLIERS. WHEN YOU MAKE DOLLHOUSE
DOLLS THE SLIP (LIQUID CLAY) IS LEFT IN THE
MOLD FOR ONLY A MINUTE AT THE MOST, THEN
THE SURPLUS IS POURED OUT. THE THICKNESS OF
THE CAST IN THE MOLD IS DETERMINED BY THE
LENGTH OF TIME THE SLIP IS LEFT IN THE MOLD
BEFORE DECANTING. IF THE SLIP IS DECANTED
AFTER ABOUT A MINUTE, THE CAST WILL BE
SUFFICIENTLY THICK TO BE HANDLED WHEN IT IS
REMOVED FROM THE MOLD AFTER ABOUT 20
MINUTES. REMEMBER THAT EVERY TIME YOU USE
A MOLD YOU ARE WEARING IT OUT A LITTLE,
ALTHOUGH YOU SHOULD GET BETWEEN 20 AND 30
HEADS FROM A GOOD MOLD.

YOU WILL NEED

- Molds for head, arms and legs
- Large, soft brush
- Rubber bands
- Plastic tray 9 × 12 inches
- Commercially prepared slip (liquid porcelain) for dollhouse dolls
- Boiled water
- Large, clean jug
- Wooden spoon
- Timer
- Paintbrushes (nos. 0000, 000, 00 and 1)
- Tissues
- Scalpel or craft knife
- Sharp pencil or toothpicks
- Underglaze paints and gloss paints
- Fine sandpaper
- Old nylon stockings or nylons
- Kiln

~ PREPARING SLIP ~

Slip is liquid clay, and it is sold in 1 gallon 3 pint plastic containers by many doll suppliers and some potteries. There are several colors to choose from, and the quality is consistently good. It also has a long shelf-life. To prepare slip for making heads, arms and legs for doll's house dolls, you must make sure that all the containers you are going to use are scrupulously clean.

Empty the slip from its container into a bucket and mix it with a wooden spoon or with your hands. If you use your hands, wear rubber gloves, because the clay will make your skin very dry. Fasten two thicknesses of muslin or old nylon stockings over the top of the original container and pour the mixed slip back. Leave to stand for an hour so that any air bubbles rise to the surface. The slip is then ready to be used.

When you have poured off the quantity you need, always clean the top of the container with a damp cloth and close it tightly. Slip dries very quickly, and if any bits are left on the rim they may fall into the clay and cause lumps or holes in the heads, arms or legs you make. Dried clay around the rim will also make it difficult to unscrew the top next time. If this happens, try knocking the container sharply with a hammer, which should loosen the clay and allow you to unscrew the top.

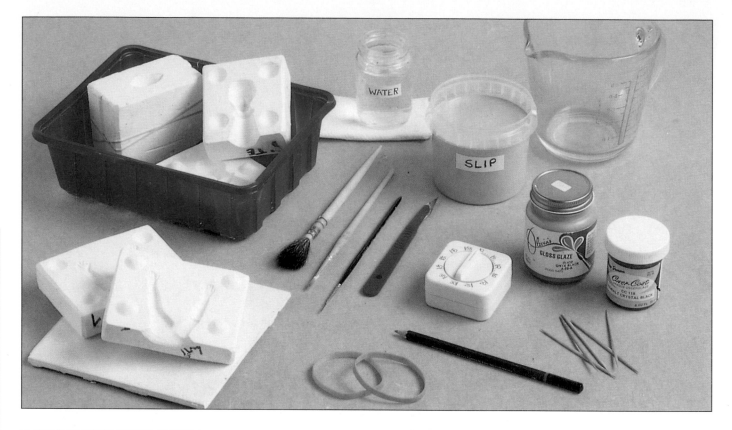

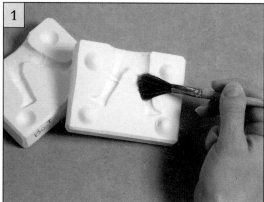

1 Clean out the molds with a soft brush. Never use a sharp tool because plaster of Paris marks easily, and all castings will show the mark, spoiling that part of all dolls you subsequently make from that mold.

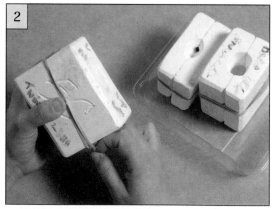

2 Hold the two halves of the mold firmly together with rubber bands and place it upright on a tray.

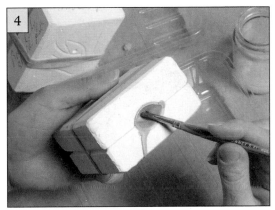

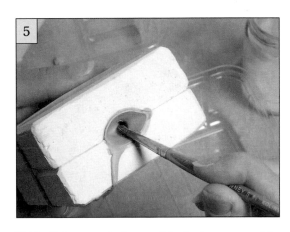

3 Pour 1¼ pints of prepared slip into a jug and add ¼ cup of boiled water. Mix thoroughly with a wooden spoon. Hold the jug fairly high and start to pour the slip in a very thin stream. At first you should aim for the edge of the tray, then, without stopping, move the jug across the molds to fill each one. Do not pause and do not worry about the small amount of clay on the tray on the outside of the molds. Try to aim the stream of slip down one side of the holes in the top of the molds so that the air can escape.

4 Leave the molds to stand for 1 minute. Decant the molds, beginning with the arms, then the legs, finally the head. Always decant the arms and hands first because the parts are so tiny that they dry out quickly. The decanted slip can be discarded. Leave the molds to drain on the tray for 15–20 minutes, propping them up against the edge of the tray. Check that the pour holes in the arms and legs are clear.

5 If the pour holes are blocked, use a no. 00 paintbrush, dipped into clean water and touch dried on a piece of tissue, to open the hole, working with a circular movement and pushing the clay away from the pour hole towards the center. This has to be done because the pipe cleaners used for the armature are inserted through these holes.

6 Carefully remove the top part of the molds. To separate the mold, place the bottom flat on the working surface, remove the rubber bands and hold the upper portion between the palms of your hands. Gently lift the top part away, making sure you lift it straight up so that you do not pull the casting out of shape. Never leave a cast piece in a mold for more than 45 minutes after decanting.

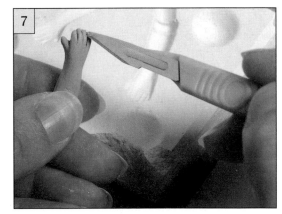

7 Carefully remove the arms from the mold. When you remove greenware from a mold, always hold the sides. If you use the pour hole you may distort the shape and it may then split when it is fired. Cut off the waste clay above the groove and clean the flash lines. Cut down between the fingers with a scalpel or craft knife. Carefully clean between the fingers with a wet paint-brush. Check that the groove around the top of the arm is sufficiently defined to hold the arm fabric in place.

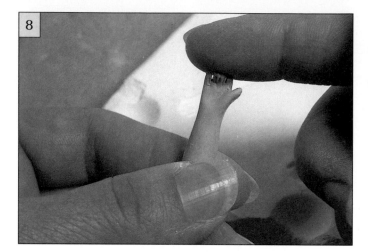

8 Delicately bend the fingers over slightly – use the handle of a paintbrush to stop them curling too far. If a finger breaks off, use a little slip to "glue" it back on. Repeat with the other hand and leave them on one side to dry.

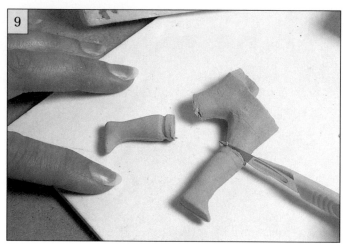

9 Remove the legs from the mold, cut away the waste clay and clean the flash lines. Hold the legs upright with the feet on a perfectly flat surface. If the legs need to be moved backwards or forwards a little, now is the time to do this.

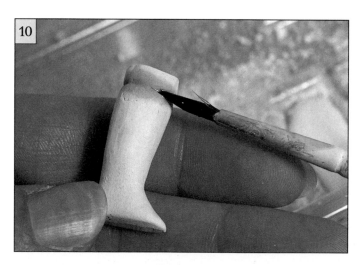

10 Make sure that the groove around the top of the leg piece is deep enough to hold the fabric securely. Use a dampened paintbrush to add definition if necessary.

11 Check the detailing on the head: the eyes, nostrils and corners of the mouth should be sharp. If you wish, add emphasis to these features with a sharp pencil or a toothpick stick, although, if the mold was good this will not be necessary. Also check that the ears are well defined. Clean away the flash lines from the side of the head.

~ REMOVING FLASH LINES ~

YOU WILL NEED

- Paintbrush (no. 0)
- Scalpel or craft knife
- Bowl of clean water
- Tissues

When you remove the cast head, arms and legs from the molds, you will notice the lines running down the sides that were caused by the join in the molds. These lines can be easily removed.

Use the round, smooth handle of a paintbrush to roll away the flash lines. If the flash lines are particularly pronounced you may need to cut them away with a scalpel or craft knife. Then dampen the bristle end of the brush and dry it a little on tissue before using it to smooth over the greenware. Work on a small area, then dampen the brush again. Do not let the brush become too dry or it will pull the greenware out of shape.

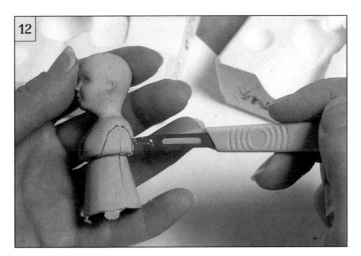

12 If you are making a shoulder-plate doll, use a scalpel or craft knife to cut away the line of the shoulder-plate.

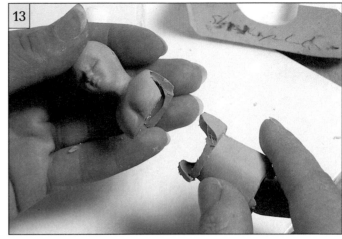

13 Carefully separate the shoulder-head from the rest of the mold, making sure you do not distort it.

~ WARNING ~

Clay dust can be harmful to your health so it is necessary to take some precautions.

Always work in a well-ventilated room with, if possible, good dust extraction equipment. You will need ready access to water and impermeable, easily-cleaned working surfaces. It is also a good idea to wear some kind of protective clothing. All cleaning must be done with the wet method. Dust should not be blown away but rather wiped away with a damp cloth.

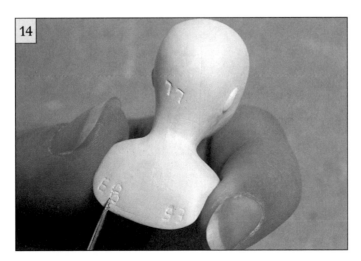

14 Remember to make an incised mark on the back of the head if it is a flange-neck doll or on the base of the shoulder-plate. You should put the date and some form of identification such as your initials. Leave the head to dry.

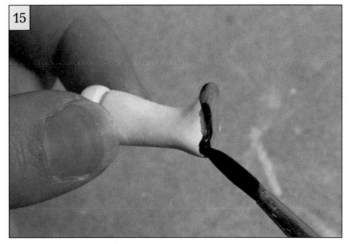

15 Use gloss underglaze paint for the stockings and shoes. Many dollhouse dolls have black shoes or boots, but you can use any color you wish. The paint will withstand firing at 2230°. When the legs are dry, gently smooth the open end with fine sandpaper so that the legs will stand upright in the kiln.

~ HOBBY KILNS ~

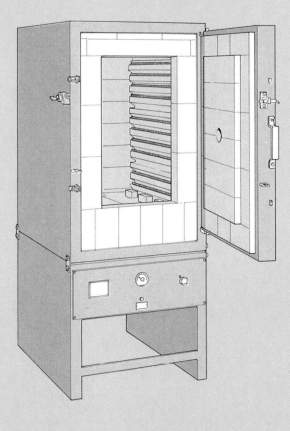

BELOW A typical electric kiln fitted with a series of elements that radiate heat. There is an automatic switch-off device if the kiln is opened during firing.

A hobby kiln is like a small oven and is just as easy to use. The firing chamber need not be larger than 9 inches wide and deep or, if it is circular, 12 inches across. Kilns can be loaded from the top or from the front. The round kilns are usually top-loading models and are generally on casters so that they can be moved. The square, front-loading kilns are too heavy to move and have to be installed in position when they are first delivered. Whichever kind of kiln you have, it must always be perfectly level because doll parts move during firing and may fall over.

Kilns can be controlled manually or automatically, and although the automatic kilns are expensive the outlay will be worthwhile if you intend to use it regularly. Many of the smaller kilns work off a 13 amp domestic electricity supply, and you should place your kiln as near as possible to a socket so that there are no trailing electric leads. The models with thermostats can be timed to switch off automatically once the correct temperature is reached. Kiln-setter type kilns are sold with full instructions and all the necessary furniture. They require special mini-bar cones. You will also need sand or kiln wash, a ceramic blanket and ceramic paper.

Modern electric kilns are fitted with safety devices that shut off the power when the kiln door is opened.

Before you stack the kiln, check the position of the thermocouple. This is the temperature unit that turns off the kiln when it is the correct temperature. It is made of a ceramic material around a wire, and it can be easily broken if, for example, it is accidentally knocked by fired bisque. Even if it is broken, the kiln is still usable because the wire in the thermostat will still control the temperature.

~ FIRING GREENWARE ~

Although each kiln will come with instructions about firing, there are really only three important points to remember:

- The greenware must be absolutely bone dry
- There should be some sand on the shelf because porcelain moves slightly during firing
- The greenware must not touch any other piece in the kiln

I always then fire on high, right from the start. You can prevent the porcelain from sticking to the floor and shelves of the kiln by using fine silica sand, a kiln wash, a ceramic blanket or ceramic paper.

Before you use the kiln, make sure that it is switched off at the plug. If you have a Kiln-setter type kiln, check that you have the correct mini-bar cone; you will need no. 6 cones for 2230° and no. 018 for 1350°. Cover the shelf or shelves with sand and stack the items of greenware, making sure that they do not touch each other. Close the kiln door and, if you have an automatic kiln, select the correct temperature and switch on. The actual firing is determined by the size of the kiln and can take 1–3 hours. You will then have to leave it for a further 5–7 hours to cool down.

~ FIRING PAINT ~

Clean all the sand from inside the kiln. This can be kept and re-used. Place all the painted heads and hands so that they are not touching and, if you have painted shoes, make sure that they are supported so that the painted area does not touch the shelf. Select the correct temperature or cone and continue as above, although this firing will take less time.

16 Dampen the eye area of the head with a paintbrush. Mix some black underglaze paint with sufficient water to make the paint just runny. Alternatively, you can wet the eyelid and add paint. Using a no. 0000 paintbrush and holding the head upside down, begin at the outside edge and paint eyelashes on the upper lid. Turn the head upside down to complete the other eye. If you make a mistake, you can use a scalpel to scrape the paint off, although you have to do this very gently and carefully. If you prefer, wait until after the bisque firing to add eyelashes.

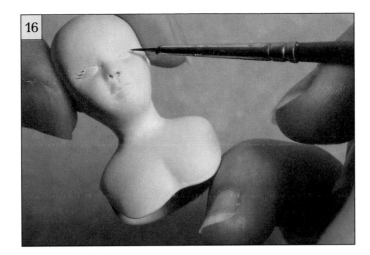

17 The greenware must be bone dry before it is fired, which can take 1–2 days. If necessary, you can place it in a conventional oven for about 1 hour at 212°. When it is dry you may wish to smooth the cheeks by rubbing them very gently with a piece of old nylon stocking or nylons wrapped around a finger. Place the heads, arms and legs inside the kiln. If you have painted boots and shoes on the legs, you must support them so that the paint does not touch the sand. If this happens, the sand will fuse with the paint and you will never be able to remove it. Greenware should be fired at 2230°.

18 After the first firing you must allow at least 4 hours for the items to cool, although this will depend on the type of kiln you have. As you can see, the fired objects are approximately 20 per cent smaller than they were when you put them in the kiln.

~ PAINTING THE MOLDED ~ HEAD

After the first kiln firing you will need to paint the head, arms and legs. It is important to give the dolls a good color because they are so small that when they are dressed and wigged their little faces will disappear if they are too pale.

One of the great advantages of painting on fired clay is the ease with which the paint can be removed if you make a mistake. The complete face can be wiped off with a tissue dipped in white spirit, while an eyelash can be removed with a dot of white spirit on the point of a paintbrush. Always wipe your cleaning brush carefully on tissue before you use it again so that you do not discolor or smudge the area you are cleaning.

You must also remember that the paint will be wet until it is fired. Handling a head so that you do not smudge the paint you have just applied requires practice. However, you can overcome this problem by firing the head after every stage of the painting process, and some people prefer to do this.

YOU WILL NEED

- Scrubber (a piece of foam with a thin layer of emery cloth glued to one side)
- Brushing medium
- Ceramic tile or saucer
- Tissues
- Wooden toothpicks
- Spatula to mix paint
- China paints
- Paintbrushes (nos. 0000, 00 and 1)
- Paintbrush (no. 000) with the bristles trimmed to about ⅛ inch long
- White spirit
- Pounce (a tiny piece of cotton wool or similar stuffing wrapped in a small piece of silk)
- Forceps
- Turpentine
- Copaiba medium

1   Use the scrubber to rub the head, hands and feet until they are perfectly smooth. You may need to rub very hard. Rinse and dry thoroughly. Place a drop of brushing medium on the tile or in a saucer and use the tip of a finger to rub it all over the face and hair (if the hair is molded), the arms and legs. Wipe it all off with a tissue. The brushing medium will make the paint go on smoothly. Use a toothpick to put a minute amount of Pompadour red on the tile and use the spatula to mix it with a tiny amount of brushing medium.

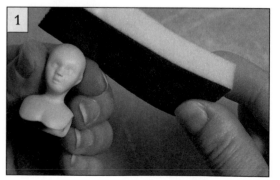

2 Use a no. 0000 paintbrush to put a dot of the paint and brushing medium mix on each cheek, then, with the cut-off paintbrush and using a circular movement, smooth the paint evenly over the cheeks. Take care that there is no harsh line between the cheeks and the neck. Keep your cut-off brush only for smoothing color on the cheeks. Do not dip it into the paint.

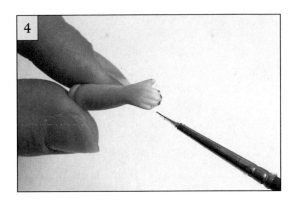

3 Put dots of red in the nose (for the nostrils) and in the corners of the eyes. Use a no. 0000 paintbrush to outline the lips, then pull the brush to the center. Pat the mouth lightly with a tissue and paint again if necessary. The top lip should be slightly darker than the lower lip.

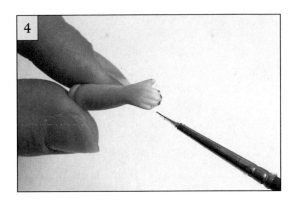

4 If you wish, you can outline the bed of the fingernails with a thin red line. Clean your brush thoroughly in white spirit and, if you wish, place tiny spots of color on the arms, wrists and knees. Pounce these until they are very light. When they are painted and to keep them from getting smudged, put the arms and legs back in the kiln, ready for firing with the head.

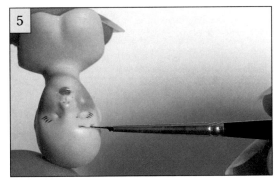

5 Paint the eyebrows with a no. 0000 paintbrush dipped in matt walnut brown. You will probably find it easier to paint the thin line if you hold the head upside down. Remember that the eyebrows should be just above the eyes and not near to the hairline. If you make a mistake, wipe the paint off with a tissue dipped in a trace of white spirit. With practice, you will be able to remove paint from under or above the eyebrow.

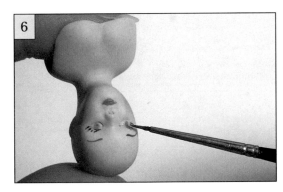

6 Paint the eyeball in white gloss paint. This is difficult to see, but is just visible if you hold the head to the light. If you wish, add a spot of color to represent the iris, although this is generally not necessary because the eyes are so small. If you add color, make sure that both eyes "look" in the same direction.

~ TIPS ~

- When you paint the white of the eye, add a drop of red food coloring to the gloss paint so that you can see what you are doing more easily. Although this makes the doll look as if it has got conjunctivitis, the red dye will be burned out during the firing.
- You may find it helpful to draw the eyebrows on in pencil as a guide before you paint them in. The pencil line will be burned out during the firing.
- If the doll's head has molded hair, mix some walnut brown or other suitable color with copaiba medium. The paint will dry quickly and can be handled, with care, before firing. Use only a tiny amount of copaiba and "pounce" the hair area to prevent the color running down the doll's neck.
- Use an old scrubber to rub over the head to give it a smooth finish. The porcelain of a well-made doll has a satiny feel.

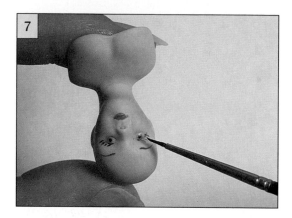

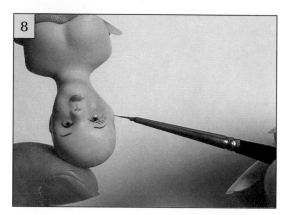

7 Use forceps to place the head in the kiln with the arms and legs ready to be refired at 1350°. When they are cool, remove the porcelain pieces from the kiln. Use black gloss to paint a fine line at the top edge of the eyeball. Take off any excess paint with a brush dipped in turpentine. The line must be as fine as you can possibly make it.

8 If you did not paint eyelashes at the greenware stage, do it now, although it has to be said that very few people bother to paint eyelashes on a dollhouse doll. Use matt black paint and a no. 0000 paintbrush. Hold the head upside down and begin at the outside edge of the upper right eyelid. Paint no more than four lashes and do not paint any below the eye. Turn the head the right side up to paint the lashes on the other eye. Any errors can be wiped away with a spot of white spirit on your no. 00 cleaning brush, which should be wiped almost dry so that the paint for the next lash does not run. When you are satisfied with the lashes, clean your brush and use gloss black paint to add a pupil to each eye. Remember that the pupil should be nearer the upper lid; centrally placed pupils will give the doll a "staring" look. Clean the brush in turpentine.

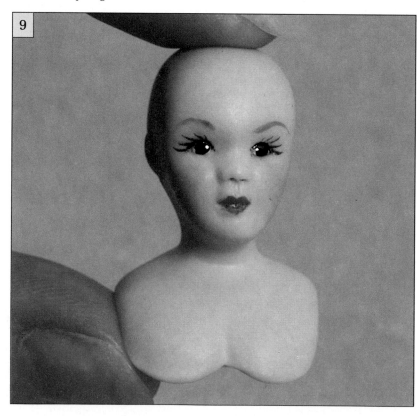

9 Use forceps to place the head in the kiln and fire again at 1350°. Heads can be fired as often as you wish provided that you do not exceed a temperature of 1350°. The finished head is now ready to be fitted to a body and dressed in the style of your choice.

MODELING A DOLL

~

MAKING A DOLL FROM YOUR OWN DESIGN AND IN YOUR OWN MOLD IS, MANY DOLL-MAKERS FEEL, THE BEST WAY. NOT ONLY IS IT GREAT FUN, BUT IT IS A FORM OF "ONE-UPMANSHIP" OVER OTHER DOLL-MAKERS WHO USE COMMERCIALLY MADE MOLDS AND KITS. WITH PRACTICE AND PERSEVERANCE YOU WILL FIND THAT YOU WILL BE ABLE TO CREATE A HUGE RANGE OF FIGURES – OLD, YOUNG, PRETTY OR UGLY – SO THAT YOU CAN FILL YOUR DOLLHOUSE WITH GENERATIONS OF A FAMILY.

I HAVE USED SUPER SCULPEY, ALTHOUGH OTHER KINDS OF CRAFT MODELING CLAY ARE AVAILABLE. ASK IN YOUR CRAFT STORE ABOUT THE ALTERNATIVES. YOU CAN MAKE PLASTER MOLDS FROM UNCURED SCULPEY, WHICH MEANS THAT THE SAME PIECE OF CLAY CAN BE USED AS THE BASIS OF SEVERAL MOLDS. YOU CAN ALSO COMBINE IT WITH OTHER MATERIALS SUCH AS ARMATURE WIRE, PLASTIC, PAPER, METAL, CLOTH, WOOD AND GLASS.

THE INSTRUCTIONS THAT FOLLOW DESCRIBE HOW TO MAKE A MOLD WITH MODELING CLAY AND PLASTER OF PARIS. HOWEVER, IF YOU WOULD PREFER TO USE THE MODELING CLAY TO MAKE A ONE-OFF DOLL, USE THE CLAY HEAD, ARMS AND LEGS FOR THE DOLL ITSELF. DUST THE CHEEKS WITH CAKE ROUGE THEN STAND THE HEAD, ARMS AND LEGS ON A TILE AND CURE THE INDIVIDUAL PARTS ACCORDING TO THE INSTRUCTIONS ON THE PACKET. PAINT THEM WITH ACRYLIC PAINTS WHEN THEY ARE COOL.

YOU WILL NEED

- Super Sculpey or similar modeling clay
- Modeling tools (you can use ordinary modeling tools or a variety of items – e.g., wooden toothpicks; manicure tools; paintbrushes)
- Plastic or marble board on which to roll clay
- "Pearl" beads
- Cake rouge

- Scissors
- Small drinking straw
- Pencil
- Plasticine
- Plastic rolling pin or straight-sided glass bottle
- Plaster of Paris
- Plastic container
- Craft knife or scalpel

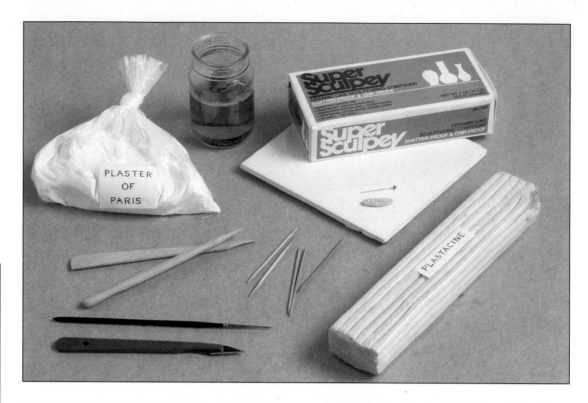

~ USING MODELING CLAY ~

When you come to mold a modeling clay such as Sculpey, it should be soft enough to mold but firm enough to hold its shape. If it is too soft, wrap a piece in foil and place it in a conventional oven at 120° for about 5 minutes. This slight heating will begin the chemical reaction that will make the clay firmer. If it is left in the oven for too long it will be too firm to use. Hard clay requires a lot of kneading before it becomes workable, although it does hold its shape well if you are making large objects.

Sculpey remains pliable until it is baked in a conventional oven, when it acquires a plastic-like hardness. To cure it completely, place it on an ovenproof dish or tile and bake at 275° for 15 minutes. If you are using other types of modeling clay, follow the manufacturer's instructions.

Provided it does not get too warm, Sculpey has a shelf-life of several years.

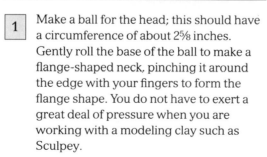

1 Make a ball for the head; this should have a circumference of about 2⅝ inches. Gently roll the base of the ball to make a flange-shaped neck, pinching it around the edge with your fingers to form the flange shape. You do not have to exert a great deal of pressure when you are working with a modeling clay such as Sculpey.

2 Divide the front of the face into quarters with a wooden toothpick or something similar.

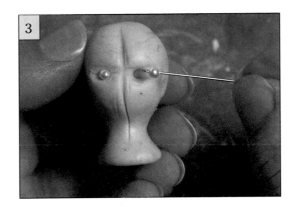

3 Use a rounded wooden tool – the end of a paintbrush, for example – to make indentations for the eye sockets. These should be just under the horizontal line and evenly spaced on either side of the vertical line. Because this head is going to be used as a mold, tiny "pearl" beads have been used. They give a smooth surface, which is easy to paint, and the plaster of Paris does not stick to them. Use a pin through the hole in the bead to position the beads. You must push them well in so that they don't protrude. If you cannot get beads use little balls of modeling clay. Beads can be used if you are making a one-off doll; they can be painted with oil paints very satisfactorily.

4 Roll out tiny pieces of clay. Add one to the chin, a tiny ball for the nose, two minute pieces for the mouth and a small piece on the forehead.

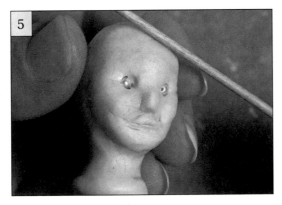

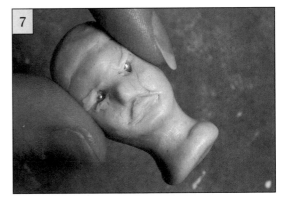

5 Smooth all the added pieces by rolling over them with a wooden toothpick. Add tiny balls of clay, slightly flattened, to both cheeks and smooth them gently.

6 Roll out two tiny pieces of clay for the ears and make them resemble tiny question marks. Put them in position, making sure they are level, then add two small balls inside the ears. Smooth over.

7 Gently squeeze the sides of the head and also manipulate the back of the head to make it more rounded. To make a shoulder-plate head add a ball of clay to the base of the neck and model it into shape, making sure that you smooth over the join with a toothpick or some similar tool.

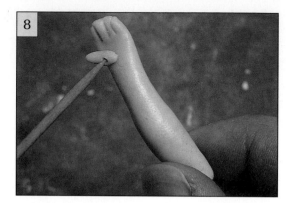

8 Prepare the hands by rolling out a piece of clay 1½ inches long and a tiny piece for the thumb. Flatten one end of the roll to make a hand and cut fingers with a pair of scissors. Separate the fingers with a toothpick, round the ends and push them back together again. Add the thumb and smooth it into the palm. Mark the nails with a tiny drinking straw. Make a groove at the top of the arm into which the fabric can be pressed. If the arm is to be used on a doll, curve over the fingers slightly; otherwise leave them straight. Make the second arm, remembering to make one left hand and one right.

9 Make a leg by rolling out a piece of clay 2 inches long. Flatten one end to form a foot and ankle and cut out toes, making sure they are not too large. Remember to make a big toe. Make a groove at the top of the leg into which the fabric can be pressed. Make the second leg in the same way, remembering to make one left leg and one right.

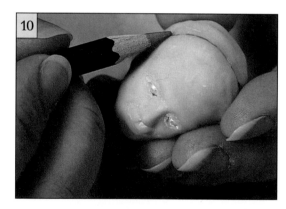

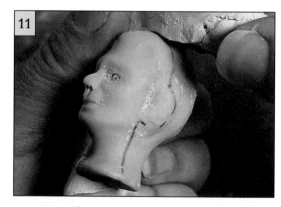

10 Take the head and draw a line right round it, making sure that you go across the highest point of the head and cheeks and exactly bisect the flange neck.

11 Use the rolling pin or bottle to roll out a strip of plasticine or Playdo about ½ × 1 × 5 inches. The strip should reach right around the head, along the line, meeting under the flange neck or shoulder-plate. Build up plasticine up to this first strip until the back of the head is embedded. To make a pour hole, shape a plug from plasticine to fill the flange neck and to meet the outside edge.

12 Continue to build up the plasticine until it lies flat on your work surface and is ½–1 inch wider than the clay model. Flatten out strips of plasticine with a rolling pin or bottle and press them around the sides of the base, smoothing them on the work surface. Build up the sides of the walls until they are at least 1 inch higher than the tip of the nose.

13 If you have used a modeling clay such as Sculpey or used other plastic modelling clay, plaster of Paris will not adhere to the surface of the pattern. However, if you have used ceramic or wood, you must paint the surface with a release agent such as clay slip or detergent.

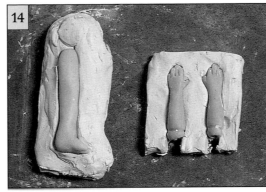

14 Prepare the plasticine beds for the arms and legs in the same way, building up the level of plasticine in readiness for the plaster of Paris.

~ TIPS ~

- Mix the plaster of Paris in a large plastic container in the proportions of 1 part water to 3 parts plaster. Always add plaster to water. Stir gently so that you do not introduce bubbles of air.
- Always use plastic containers when you are working with plaster of Paris. When the plaster has dried it can be easily knocked off the surface.
- If your doll looks too large and out of scale, make another mold of the fired head, remembering to paint it with a release agent before you pour in the plaster of Paris.

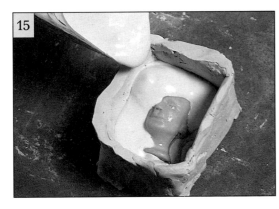

15 Mix the plaster of Paris and when it begins to resemble the consistency of thick cream, pour it down the side of the plasticine surround, filling the area to the top. Leave for 15–20 minutes. Remove the plasticine base and wall from the back of the pattern. Do not part the pattern and plaster. Use a small coin or something similar to make some indentations in the plaster while it is still soft; these will act as key marks so that both halves of the plaster mold align exactly. Rebuild the plasticine walls around your model. Coat the model and, especially, the plaster, with a release agent. Remember to make a plug for the pour hole and seal the plasticine carefully around the base and in the corners. Mix fresh plaster and, when it begins to thicken, pour it into the plasticine surround. Leave for 20 minutes.

16 Remove the plasticine surround. Place the mold in a bowl of water for 3–5 minutes and pry apart gently. If necessary, enlarge the size of the pour hole with a craft knife. Leave to dry for 1–2 days; alternatively, place in a conventional oven at 212° for 1 hour. When the molds are completely dry, they are ready for you to use to make your own dolls with slip (see the previous project).

DRESSING DOLLHOUSE DOLLS

Clothes for tiny dolls can be easily hand sewn. They are not at all difficult to make once you have grasped the basic techniques and have got in the habit of "thinking small".

The costumes in this book will give you basic patterns for costumes ranging from the early Victorian period to the Edwardian era. Most of the patterns included in this book are interchangeable. Adapting them to make them appropriate for different periods can be simply done by making slight changes to the basic pattern – lengthening or shortening skirts or jackets, for example, or altering details such as lace trims or hats. It is often the accessories and details of decoration and color that give a flavor of a period more successfully than the most elaborate of costumes. There are many good, illustrated books on costume, fabrics and accessories available, and for most styles it will be unnecessary to do any special research. However, if you are planning to dress a doll as a particular person or with an especially ornate costume or elaborate hair style you may need to do a little extra research.

A great many dollhouse dolls have nothing to their bodies but a few pieces of wire covered by bandage-type fabric and a little polyester stuffing. Most have underclothes that are either glued or attached to the body with adhesive or a few stitches. This is fine if the dolls are going to be static in a dollhouse or even in a framed picture as part of a tableau. It is, too, the easiest way for a lot of people to begin dressing dolls. However, more often than not, dolls are turned upside down when they are admired and looked at, and for this reason I have added pantaloons and a "pretend petticoat" to the clothes for all the lady dolls.

The silhouette of the finished dolls is important, and it is achieved in two main ways – by the hair style and the line of the top clothes. Wigs should be small and appropriate for the time and place – far too many dolls have so much hair that their faces are barely visible. Because the overall line is so important, unnecessary seams and gathers, which add unwanted volume, have been eliminated from the patterns.

You will already have to hand most of the sewing equipment you will need – sharp pointed scissors, fine needles, pins and so forth. Because turning up hems can create unattractive bulk on these tiny clothes, I have advised you to use one of the polyamide bonding webs that are widely available from haberdashers and department stores. These are made in a range of widths under different trade-names, including Vilene and Wundaweb, and they are easy to use. Simply cut off an appropriate length of the web, insert it between the two fabrics to be joined and press firmly with a hot, dry iron under a damp cloth. Leave to cool for about 10 minutes. Alternatively, use hot glue stitch powder, which is also ironed on. Place a piece of greaseproof paper over the material to protect the heel of your iron if you use this. It is useful to keep a bottle of a proprietary "fray check" to hand.

I have recommended that you use a clear, all-purpose adhesive to attach some of the trims and lace edgings. I have also suggested that you may sometimes want to glue a dress to the doll, although, because almost all of the patterns are designed to be removed so that you can dress and redress your dolls, it is better to attach the clothes with one or two small stitches. Almost all of the patterns are lined, which eliminates rough edges, and include a ¼ inch seam allowance.

5

VICTORIAN
LADY

~

THIS IS ONE OF THE EASIEST WAYS TO DRESS A
DOLL. WHEN THE DOLL IS TURNED UPSIDE
DOWN, THE LACE-EDGED PANTALOONS AND
TRIMMED UNDERSKIRT GIVE THE IMPRESSION
THAT THE DOLL HAS A FULL SET OF
UNDERCLOTHES. THE PATTERN CAN BE EASILY
ADAPTED FOR OTHER DOLLS. YOU COULD, FOR
EXAMPLE, MAKE IT IN PLAIN FABRIC WITH
MATCHING OR CONTRASTING LACE TRIM AND USE
IT TO DRESS A GRANDMOTHER DOLL.

YOU WILL NEED

- Tracing paper
- Pencil
- Pins
- Scissors
- Narrow bonding web
- Needle
- Sewing thread
- Forceps or tweezers
- Sewing machine (optional)

FOR THE PANTALOONS

- 6 inches white cotton lawn
- 6 inches white edging lace, ¼ inch wide
- Shirring elastic (optional)

FOR THE DRESS

- 9 inches white cotton lawn
- 18 inches delicately patterned soft cotton or silk
- 12 inches white edging lace, ¼ inch wide
- 36 inches gathered white edging lace, 1 inch wide
- All-purpose adhesive

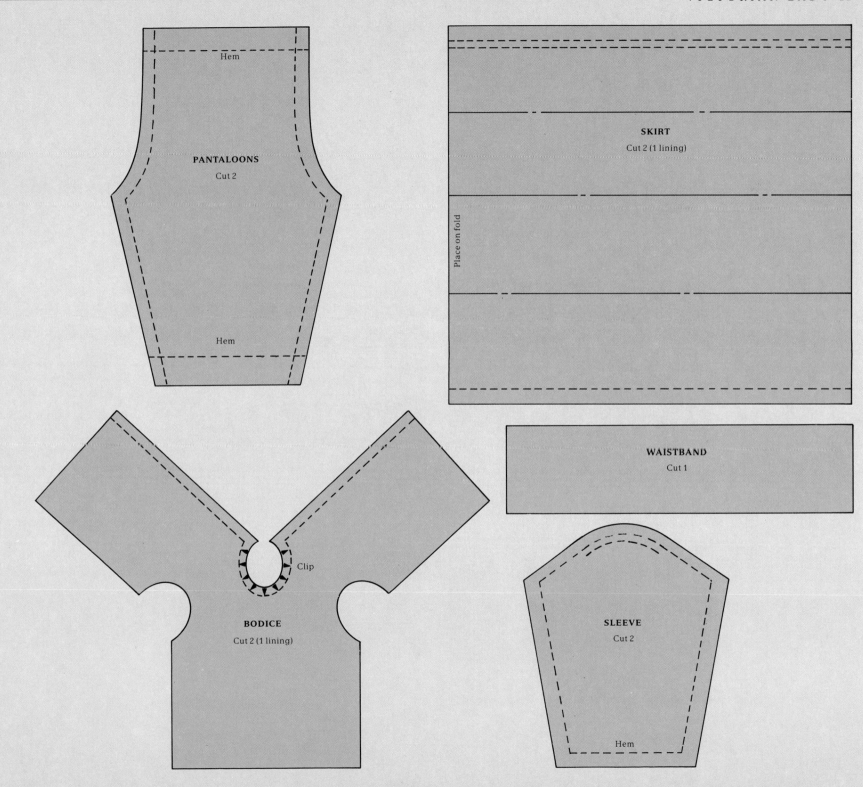

PANTALOONS
Cut 2

Hem

Hem

SKIRT
Cut 2 (1 lining)

Place on fold

WAISTBAND
Cut 1

BODICE
Cut 2 (1 lining)

Clip

SLEEVE
Cut 2

Hem

1 Cut out two pieces and stitch the center front seam, with a turning allowance of ¼ inch.

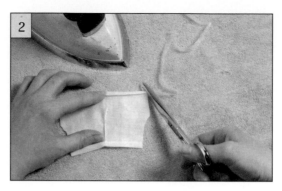

2 Press open the seam and turn down the waist and leg hem allowance with narrow bonding web.

3 Pin and stitch narrow lace along the bottom edge.

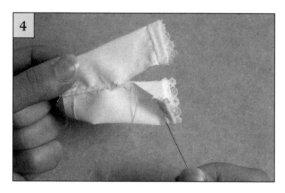

4 Turn right sides together and stitch the center back seam.

5 Stitch the inner leg seam, catching in the raw ends of the lace.

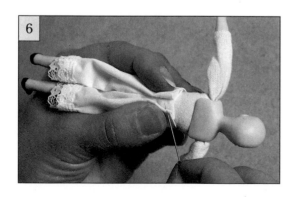

6 Make a row of small running stitches around the top. Dress the doll in the pantaloons and gather them up tightly around the waist. Stitch the top of the pantaloons to the doll's body. Alternatively, the top hem can be turned down and stitched and fine elastic threaded through. Tie the elastic tightly to finish.

7 The finished pantaloons. All lady dolls wear pantaloons of this pattern, although the length of leg varies. The maids, cook, grandmother and girl all wear the same style.

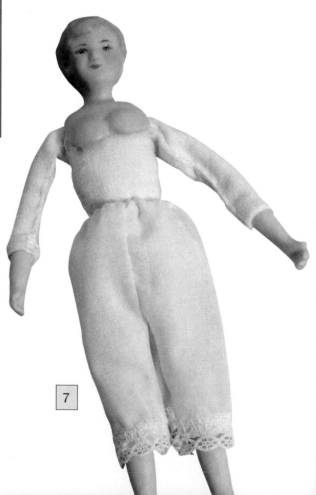

MAKING
— THE —
BODICE

1 Cut out two sleeves in patterned cotton and two dress top pieces, one in patterned cotton and one in white lawn. Stitch according to marks on pattern.

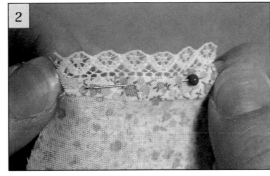

2 Use bonding web to turn up the bottom hem of the sleeves, and then pin and stitch narrow lace around the wrist edge.

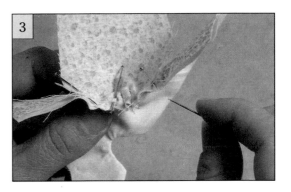

3 With right sides together, stitch the bodice pieces together. Clip around the neck seam. Turn to the right side and press the seams flat. Stitch the sleeve to the armhole.

4 Stitch the sleeve top to the shoulder, easing the fullness at the top to fit.

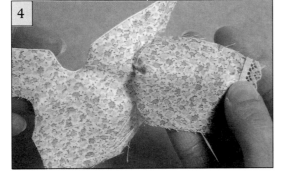

5 Put the bodice, with the lining outwards, on the doll. Pin at the back of the neck and the waist, then pin the underarm seams and side seams to check for fit.

6 Remove the pins from the neck and waist and carefully take off the bodice. Stitch the wrist to waist seam, making an allowance of ¼ inch. Trim back the seam to the stitching line, oversewing it for strength if you wish. Turn the bodice to the right side, using forceps or tweezers to turn the sleeves out.

7 Stitch two pieces of ¼ inch lace to run from the center front to the shoulders. Put the bodice on the doll and neatly oversew the back seam. To avoid unnecessary bulk around the waist, do not hem the lower edge of the bodice.

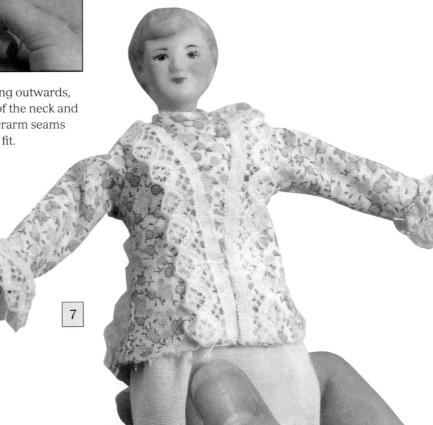

MAKING THE SKIRT

1 Cut out two skirt pieces, one in patterned cotton and one in cotton lawn, remembering to place one of the shorter sides of the template against a fold of each kind of material. With right sides together, machine or hand stitch around three sides, leaving the waist edge open.

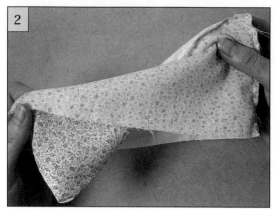

2 Turn to the right side. Press lightly to neaten the sewn edges.

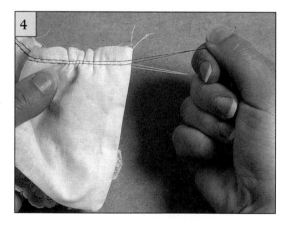

3 Starting at the hem edge, stitch three or four layers of gathered lace around the skirt so that each row overlaps the previous row by ¼ inch.

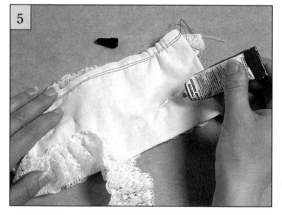

4 Stitch two parallel rows along the top edge of the skirt to gather the skirt. If you use a sewing machine, put a different color thread on the bobbin so that you can see the gathering thread more easily.

5 Glue or sew a layer of lace to the lining so that its bottom edge is perfectly level with the bottom layer of lace on the overskirt. This represents the petticoat.

6 Cut out a waistband from the patterned material. Gather the skirt to fit the doll's waist, then, with right sides together, sew the waistband to the skirt.

7 Fold over the waistband and catch it in place on the lining to neaten the top edge.

~ TIPS ~

- Always clip curved seams to the stitch line so that they lie flat when the garment is turned to the right side.
- Decorate garments with paints and add lace while the clothes are still flat. You will find it much easier to work on the tiny articles before the side seams are stitched.
- Protect the doll's hair with plastic film, held in place by a rubber band around the neck, while you dress the doll.

8 Place the skirt over the bodice, pulling the waistband tightly around the doll. Sew the waistband firmly together and slip stitch the skirt together down the back.

~ MAKING A PARASOL ~

No Victorian or Edwardian lady would be seen outside without a parasol to protect her fair skin from the sun. Parasols varied in size, but all were prettily edged with ribbons or lace.

YOU WILL NEED

- Tracing paper
- Pencil
- Scissors
- Pins
- 5 × 5 inch patterned lace
- 18 inch edging lace, ½ inch wide
- All-purpose adhesive
- 4 inch thin white plastic tube
- Pin with colored top

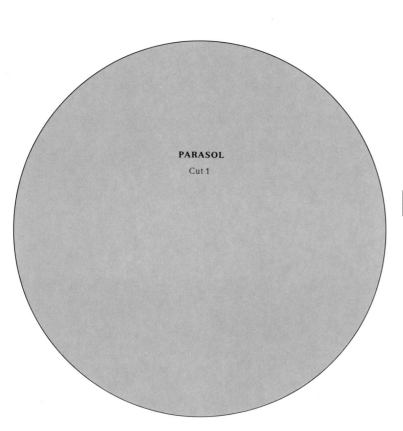

PARASOL

Cut 1

1 Place the template on the lace and cut around the edge.

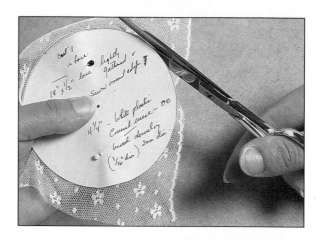

2 Either gather the lace by hand or use a pleater. Draw it up to fit the circumference of the circle and glue it in position. Fold the circle in four and place four pins to divide the circumference equally into quarters.

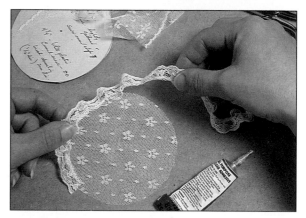

3 Make a small hole in the center of the circle and push the plastic tube through it so that about 1 inch protrudes at the top. Glue the lace to the tube around the hole. Put a little adhesive on the lower part of the tube and stick the four folded edges to the handle. Stick the pin into the bottom of the tube to act as a handle.

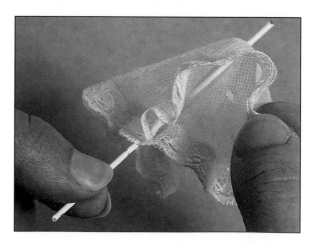

GRANDMOTHER

~

ONCE YOU HAVE MADE THE BASIC DRESS FOR
THE VICTORIAN LADY, YOU CAN EASILY ADAPT IT
FOR OTHER MEMBERS OF THE FAMILY. MAKE THE
DRESS IN A PLAIN, DARK COTTON AND DECORATE
IT WITH ONLY A LITTLE LACE AND IT WILL BE
PERFECT FOR A GRANDMOTHER. ADD A SHAWL
AND A GRAY WIG AND YOU HAVE AN IDEAL DOLL
FOR A VICTORIAN PARLOR. MAKE A LITTLE PILL-
BOX HAT WITH A FEATHER IN IT, AND SHE WILL
BE MORE SUITABLE FOR AN EARLY EDWARDIAN
DRAWING ROOM.

MAKING THE WIG

YOU WILL NEED

- All-purpose adhesive
- Scissors

FOR THE WIG

- 6 inches white mohair
- 6 inches string
- Small bulldog clip
- Setting lotion
- Needle
- White sewing thread

FOR THE HAT

- Piece of buckram, ½ inch wide, to go round doll's head
- Scraps of fabric and trimming to match doll's dress
- Feather or other decoration

FOR THE SHAWL

- Tracing paper
- Pencil
- 8 inches fine wool fabric
- Narrow bonding web
- Needle
- Thread
- 12 inches fringe to match (see box)

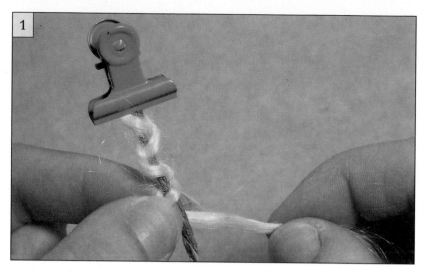

1 | Because this wig is not removable, it is best to dress the doll first. Gently brush out the mohair. Divide it into two equal bunches and hold it with a piece of string in a bulldog clip. Braid the mohair firmly around the string. Wet thoroughly with setting lotion and leave to dry.

2 | Remove the string and tease out the mohair, but do not brush it.

3 | Cover the doll's head up to the hairline with adhesive and place the mohair across the head, taking it to the back of the head but allowing the waves to fall softly around the doll's face.

4 | Twist together the long ends of hair and wind them into a bun. Use white sewing thread to hold the ends in place.

5 The finished wig. It adds instant years onto the age of the doll.

MAKING THE SHAWL

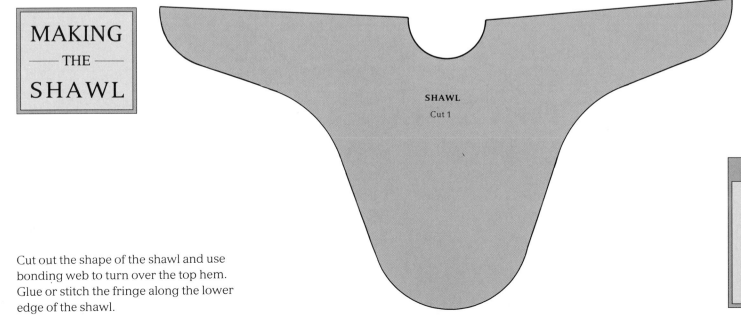

SHAWL

Cut 1

Cut out the shape of the shawl and use bonding web to turn over the top hem. Glue or stitch the fringe along the lower edge of the shawl.

~ MAKING A FRINGE ~

Trim a lady's lightweight summer shawl with a long, white fringe or add a matching fringe to a woollen shawl. Satin, which frays easily, is useful for adding fringes to clothes or even to furniture. Use scraps about 12 × 3 inches. Shawls can also be prettily finished off with a little trimming made from grosgrain ribbon.

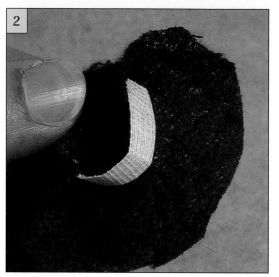

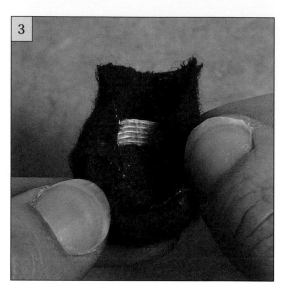

1 Measure and cut the buckram so that it sits firmly on the doll's head. Glue the ends together to form a circle.

2 Cut out a circle of fabric to match or contrast with the doll's dress and place the buckram circle in the center.

3 Glue the fabric inside the hat, trimming it as necessary so that it is not too bulky.

4 Decorate the rim of the hat with braid or lace to match the dress, gluing it in place. Decorate with a small feather if you wish.

7

VICTORIAN
MAN

~

VICTORIAN MEN ARE USUALLY DRESSED IN DARK COATS WITH PANTS OF A DIFFERENT MATERIAL – STRIPED OR CHECKED, FOR EXAMPLE – AND OFTEN WITH A FANCY WAISTCOAT. TOP HATS, WITH CROWNS OF VARIOUS HEIGHTS, WERE WORN ON ALL OCCASIONS. TO ELIMINATE UNNECESSARY BULK, SHIRTS DO NOT HAVE SLEEVES. FOR THE SAME REASON ONLY THE FRONT OF THE WAISTCOAT IS MADE AND ATTACHED TO THE SHOULDERS AND AT THE BACK. THE COAT SLEEVES ARE ATTACHED TO THE BODY AT THE SHOULDER, WHICH IS EASIER THAN FITTING THEM INTO A COAT. THE SAME BASIC PATTERN FOR THE SHIRT IS USED ON ALL MEN DOLLS WHO WEAR COATS OR JACKETS.

YOU WILL NEED

- Tracing paper
- Pencil
- Pins
- Scissors
- Narrow bonding web
- Needle
- Sewing thread
- Forceps or tweezers
- Sewing machine (optional)

FOR THE PANTS

- 9 inches checked or striped material

FOR THE SHIRT

- 12 inches white cotton lawn
- 6 inches black or blue silk or velvet ribbon, ¼ inch wide

FOR THE WAISTCOAT

- 6 inches checked or striped material (to match pants)
- 6 inches iron-on backing fabric (such as Vilene)
- Black craft paint
- Wooden toothpick
- All-purpose adhesive
- Fine chain

FOR THE FROCK COAT

- 12 inches lightweight black suiting material
- 9 inches colored satin (for lining, optional)
- 12 inches black bias binding

FOR THE TOP HAT

- Small pill box or similar of appropriate diameter for crown of hat
- Plastic film
- Rubber bands
- 8 inches black or gray felt
- 1 tbsp. PVA
- Hot water
- 3 pieces card, 3 × 1 inch
- All-purpose adhesive
- White pencil or crayon
- 1½ inches ribbon, ⅛ inch wide to match felt

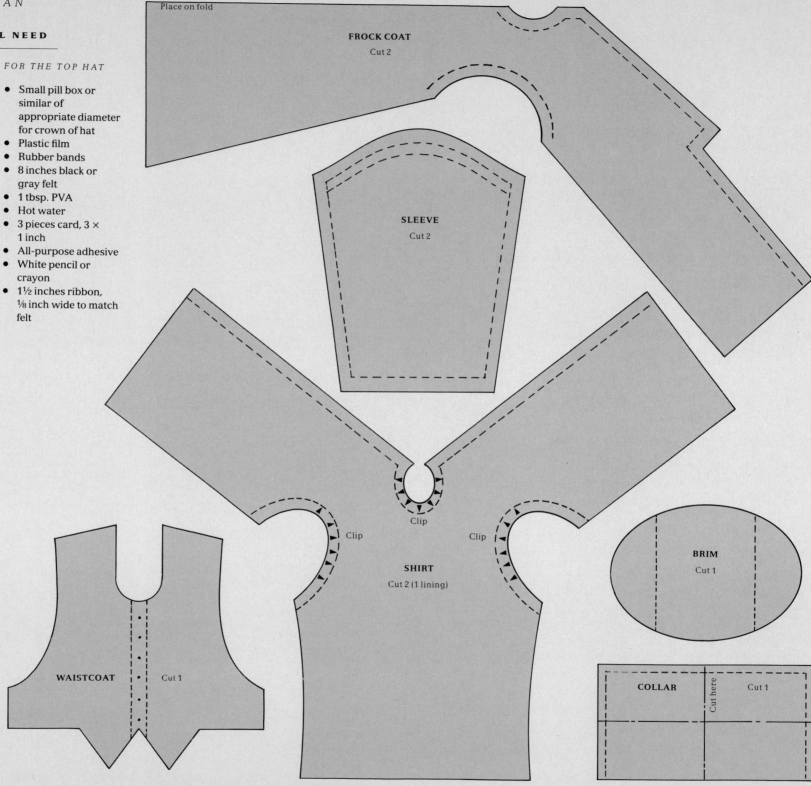

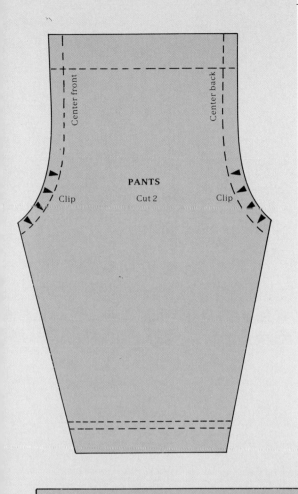

PANTS

Center front

Center back

Clip

Cut 2

Clip

CROWN OF HAT

Cut 1

MAKING
— THE —
PANTS

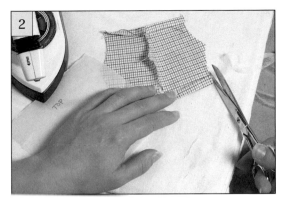

1   Cut out two pant pieces from checked or striped material and stitch the front center seam, leaving a ¼ inch seam allowance.

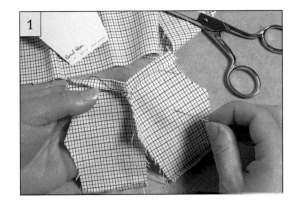

2   Use bonding web to turn up the hems at the bottom of the legs and around the waist.

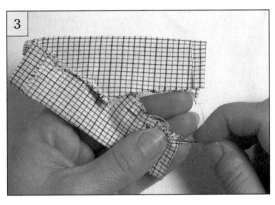

3   Turn the right sides together and stitch the center back seam. Refold, matching front and back seams. Stitch the crotch and inner leg seams.

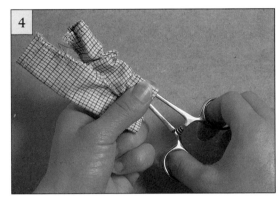

4   Use forceps or tweezers to turn the pants the right way out.

5   Press the pants and place them on the doll. Catch them with tiny stitches around the doll's waist.

MAKING
—THE—
SHIRT

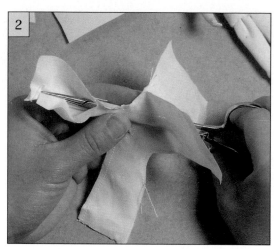

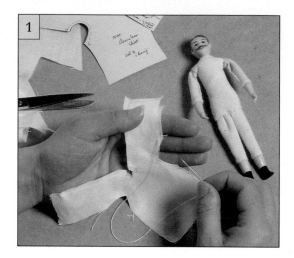

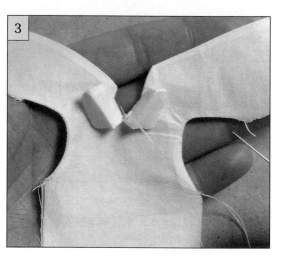

1 Cut out two shirt pieces (one as a lining) and one collar piece from white cotton lawn. Fold the collar in half lengthways and stitch the three open sides, trimming the fabric up the corner seams. Cut the collar in half, turn each piece to the right side and turn in the cut edges by hand to neaten. Press lightly and put to one side.

2 Stitch shirt piece and lining together around the underarm seams and up the center back and around the neck as shown on pattern. Clip to the stitch line and turn to the right side.

3 Press lightly to flatten the seams and stitch the collar pieces to the centre front of the neck by hand.

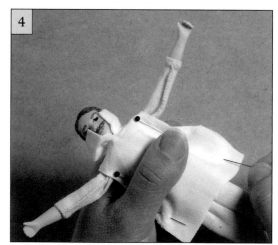

4 Put the shirt on the doll with the wrong side outwards and pin the side and back seams. Remove the pins from the back, remove the shirt and sew up the two side seams. Turn right side out and press. Put the shirt back on the doll and neatly oversew the back seam.

5 Make a tie by knotting the ribbon at the front and take the ends to the back of the neck, sewing them firmly together.

6 The finished shirt and tie.

~ ADDING SLEEVES TO THE ~ SHIRT

You may sometimes want to dress a man doll with a shirt with sleeves.

You will need

- Tracing paper
- Pins
- Pencil
- Scissors
- 6 inches white cotton lawn
- Narrow bonding web
- Needle
- Sewing thread

Cut out two sleeve pieces. Use bonding web to turn up the cuff hems and stitch the sides together. Turn to the right side. Slip the arms on the doll and catch them in place around the shoulders of the shirt body. Alternatively, slip the sleeves on the undressed doll and catch them directly to the arms before dressing the doll in the shirt body.

~ MAKING A SLEEVE BOARD ~

A sleeve board can be useful if you have to sew sleeves into a jacket or shirt when they have not been put in flat. You can also lightly press sleeves around a board so that they hold their shape, and it is often easier to add a cuff or lace trim to a sleeve before the sleeve is attached to the coat or dress. You can use a piece of wooden dowel, about 6 inches and ¼ inch in diameter or, as here, the empty plastic barrel of a ballpoint pen. You will also need approximately 8 inches of 2 inch wide bonding material and adhesive.

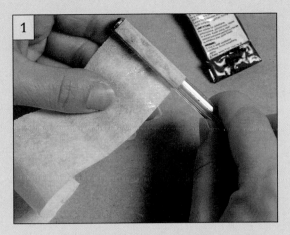

1 Wrap the bonding material around the dowel or pen, holding it down with a spot of adhesive.

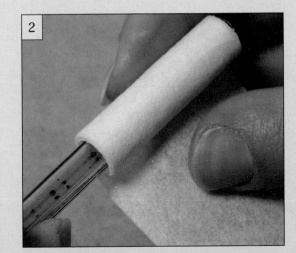

2 Continue to wrap the bonding around until the diameter is sufficient to support a sleeve but not so large that it cannot be inserted into the sleeve.

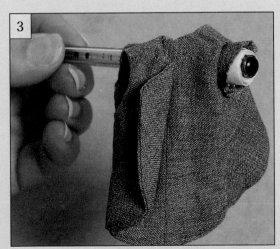

3 Finish off with a spot of adhesive and allow to dry before using.

MAKING
— THE —
WAISTCOAT

This pattern can be easily adapted to make a higher or lower neckline to suit the doll to be dressed. Once you have bonded the waistcoat material to the lining, modify the pattern as you wish before following the steps below.

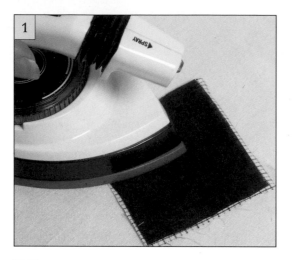

1 Fuse the backing material to the waistcoat material with an iron.

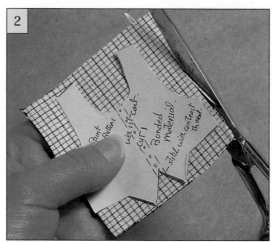

2 Cut out the waistcoat.

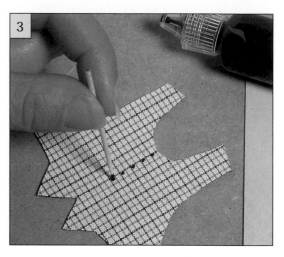

3 Use a wooden toothpick to paint on buttons down the center front of the waistcoat.

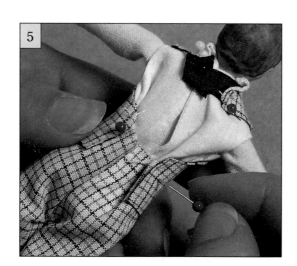

5 Place the waistcoat on the doll, pinning it in position at the shoulders and down the sides.

6 Neatly stitch the waistcoat in position.

6

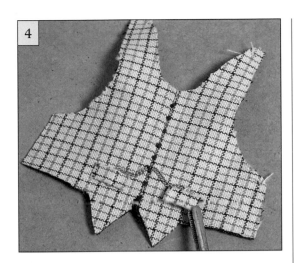

4 Cut out pocket fronts from scraps of fused fabric and glue them in position, adding a tiny length of chain running from pocket to pocket.

~ TIP ~

One way of eliminating bulk is to omit those parts of garments that are not visible. Shirt sleeves cannot be seen under a coat, for example. If you are dressing a man doll in a waistcoat, you need only make the front, which can be attached with a few tiny stitches at the shoulders and to the underarm seams of the shirt.

MAKING
— THE —
FROCK COAT

The name "frock coat" was used for several different styles. It can be a double-breasted coat with a full skirt reaching to the knees at both the front and back or it can have cut-out fronts. They are often made with lining that is the same color as the main fabric, but if you are dressing a doll for a special occasion, you might want to use a contrasting color of satin lining fabric.

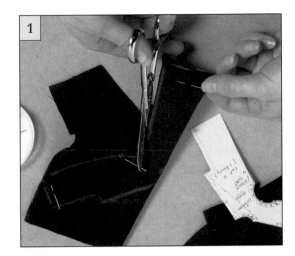

1 Cut two pieces for the coat (remembering to use a different fabric for the lining if you wish) and two sleeves, which will be attached to the doll's body, not to the coat itself.

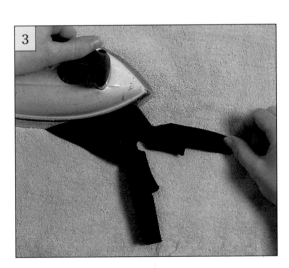

3 Turn the coat to the right side, using tweezers or forceps to pull through the material of the front, and press lightly to turn back the collar revers.

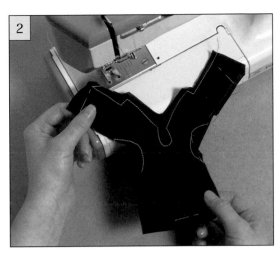

2 Machine or hand stitch the two coat pieces together around the underarm seams, and from the bottom of one front, around the neck and down the other front. Clip the arm and neck curves.

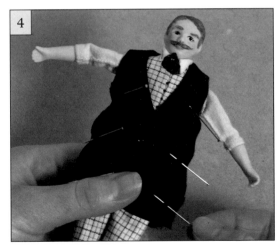

4 Dress the doll in the coat and pin the side seams together. If you have used a different colored lining, you should put the coat on inside out. Take off the coat and neatly stitch the side seams.

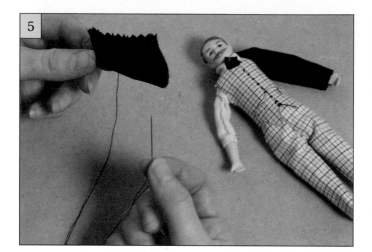

5   Use bonding web to turn up the cuff hems of the sleeves. Stitch the underarm seams and turn the sleeves the right way out.

6   Slip them onto the doll and attach them at the shoulder with a few stitches.

7   Attach black bias binding to the bottom hem of the coat, turn it under and slip stitch it to the lining.

8   Dress the doll in the coat, catching it at the shoulder of the sleeves with a few tiny stitches.

9   The dressed doll.

MAKING ── THE ── TOP HAT

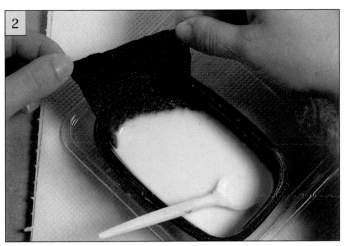

1. Cover one end of the pill box with a small piece of plastic film, holding the film in position with a rubber band.

2. Cut out one piece of felt for the crown of the hat and one piece for the brim, and soak them in the PVA mixed with hot water.

3. Pull the felt for the crown firmly down over the end of the covered pill box. Press it down as firmly as you can and hold it tightly in place with a rubber band. Leave until dry.

4. Glue the three strips of card together to make a former for the brim and cover them with plastic film. Press the soaked circle of felt firmly around the former. Leave until dry.

5. Take the crown from the pill box and cut the rubber band. Trim the felt so that the crown is about 1 inch high.

6   Place the pill box in the center of the brim and draw around it with a white pencil or crayon.

7   Punch a hole in the center of the circle you have drawn and make a series of wedge-shaped cuts out to the edge of the circle.

8   Bend up the wedges and glue them to the inside of the crown.

9   Glue a length of narrow ribbon around the bottom of the crown to cover the join with the brim.

10   The Victorian man is now ready to go out.

~ EDWARDIAN MAN ~

After you have made the Victorian man, it is really quite simple to alter the period of his dress. The Lounge Suit was especially popular in Edwardian times, so, by replacing the frock coat with a lounge jacket (see page 62) his dress becomes suitable for the time. This man has a grey morning suit which is versatile enough to be worn for many different occasions.

~ EDWARDIAN LADY ~

The outfit of the Victorian Lady can easily be altered to one that is suitable for Edwardian times. Follow the patterns and instructions for the bodice on page 40, but choose another fabric and use less lace. As Edwardian skirts vary, it is advisable to choose your own pattern. They are easily obtained. Add a wide-brimmed hat with an extravagant feather and the result is an elegant lady.

~ MAKING A LOUNGE SUIT ~ JACKET

Being able to change part of the clothing on a doll and move it to another century is an easy way of filling your dollhouse with a new family. The Victorian man is an excellent example of this. If you take off his frock coat and large tie, you can give him an ordinary lounge suit jacket, made from the same fabric as his pants and waistcoat, and he will jump forwards in time by a century. You could make him into a business man, for example, by giving him a new tie, different hat – a bowler or a homburg, perhaps – and a walking cane.

The jacket here is made from the same checked material as the pants and waistcoat, and it must, therefore, be made a little differently from the plain black frock coat. The jacket has shoulder seams.

YOU WILL NEED

- Tracing paper
- Pencil
- Pins
- Scissors
- 18 inches fabric to match pants and waistcoat
- 6 inches white cotton or lining fabric
- Needle
- Sewing thread
- Narrow bonding web
- Black craft paint
- Wooden toothpick
- Dark narrow ribbon for tie
- All-purpose adhesive

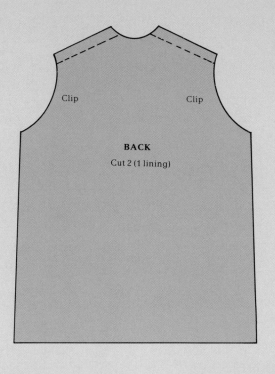

BACK
Cut 2 (1 lining)

Clip   Clip

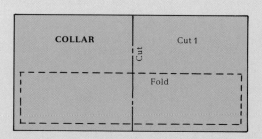

COLLAR
Cut 1

Cut

Fold

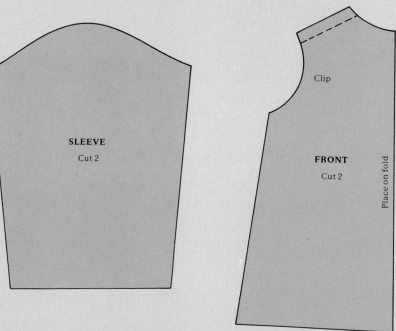

SLEEVE
Cut 2

Clip

FRONT
Cut 2

Place on fold

1 | Cut out two front pieces from the main fabric, following the direction of the pattern carefully and remembering to place the center line against a fold in the fabric. Because the front of the jacket is self-lined, you can fold back the top to form revers without having to include an extra seam.

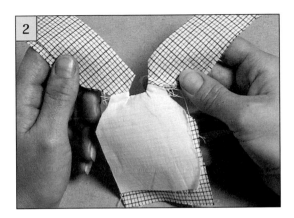

2 Cut out two back pieces, one in main fabric and one in lining. Fold the two front pieces in half and stitch all shoulder seams together, so that the back lining is attached to the front shoulders. Stitch around the neck curve, clip and turn to the right sides. Press lightly.

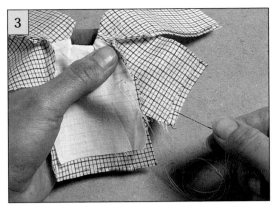

3 Cut out two sleeves from the main fabric and turn up the cuff hem with bonding web. Attach the sleeves to the jacket shoulders. At this stage the jacket is still flat.

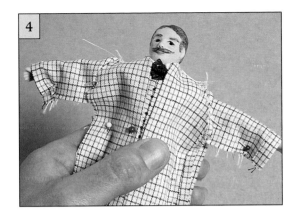

4 Still with the jacket inside out, place it on the doll and pin down the front and then pin the side and underarm seams together. Remove the front pins and stitch the underarm and side seams, starting at the cuff edge and sewing to the lower edge of the jacket. Turn the jacket to the right side. Hem the lower edge by hand. Press, turning back the revers.

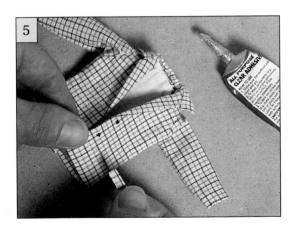

5 Cut out the back collar. Fold it in two lengthways and stitch the two short edges. Turn to the right side, turn in the long edges and stitch along the back neck of the jacket. Use a toothpick to paint on some buttons and glue little pieces of fabric in place to represent pocket flaps.

6 Dress the doll in the jacket. If you wish, give him a new tie by fastening a thin piece of ribbon around his neck under the collar of his shirt.

8

VICTORIAN GIRL

~

IN VICTORIAN AND EDWARDIAN TIMES
CHILDREN OF THE UPPER CLASSES WERE
GENERALLY DRESSED AS LITTLE ADULTS. LITTLE
GIRLS WORE LACE-EDGED PANTALOONS AND
FRILLY PETTICOATS. MANY PAINTINGS AND
PRINTS FROM THAT PERIOD SHOW DRESSES WITH
LACE, RIBBONS AND BOWS AND, EVEN ON THE
HOTTEST DAYS, COATS. LITTLE GIRLS ALSO WORE
HIGHLY DECORATED HATS. THE SET OF CLOTHES
DESCRIBED HERE IS TO FIT A DOLLHOUSE DOLL
THAT IS 3–3½ INCHES TALL.

YOU WILL NEED

- Tracing paper
- Pencil
- Pins
- Scissors
- Needle
- Sewing thread
- Narrow bonding web
- Forceps or tweezers
- Sewing machine

FOR THE PANTALOONS

- 6 inches fine white cotton fabric
- 6 inches white edging lace, ¼ inch wide

FOR THE DRESS

- 9 inches very fine white cotton fabric
- 45 inches (total) insertion lace, ½ inch wide (white or colored)
- 45 inches (total) edging lace, ¼ inch wide (white or colored)
- 6 tiny pearl beads
- All-purpose adhesive (optional)

FOR THE COAT

- 9 inches fine cotton fabric with dainty pattern (or quantity of lining fabric)
- 15 inches edging lace, ¼ inch wide (white or to match pattern)
- 15 inches edging Picot (white or to match pattern)

FOR THE BONNET

- 10 inches white insertion lace, ½ inch wide
- 10 inches white edging lace, ¼ inch wide
- Embroidered motif
- 15 inches silk ribbon, ⅛ inch wide
- Shirring elastic

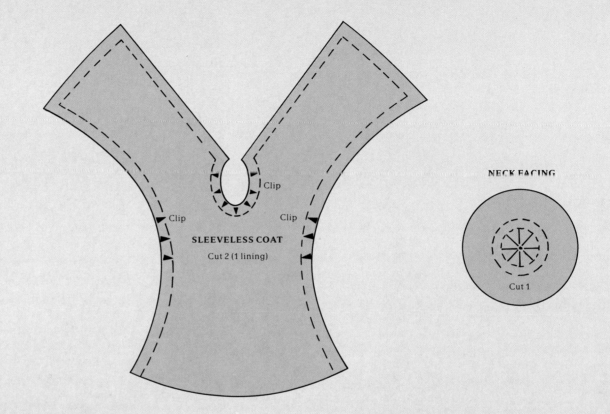

SLEEVELESS COAT
Cut 2 (1 lining)

Clip

NECK FACING

Cut 1

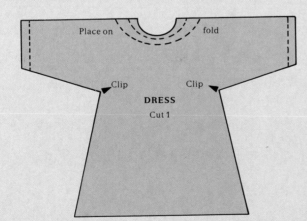

Place on fold

Clip   Clip

DRESS
Cut 1

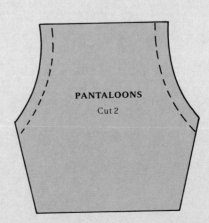

PANTALOONS
Cut 2

MAKING THE DRESS

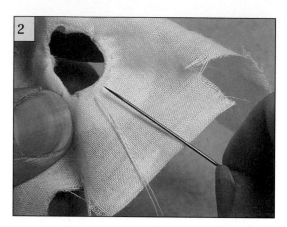

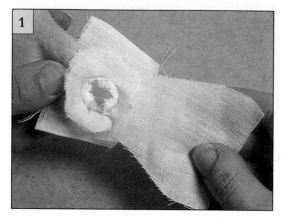

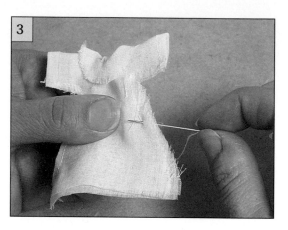

1 Before you make the dress make the pantaloons in the same way as those for the Victorian Lady (see page 42). Cut out the dress pattern and neck facing from fine white cotton fabric. Mark the center of the neck line of the dress with a pin. Baste the neck facing to the dress, using the smallest possible stitches, cut out the center of the facing and clip the edges of the circle. Try the dress on the doll. If it will not go over the doll's head, stitch another circle just outside the first circle and cut again. If the doll has a wig, you may find it easiest to remove the wig before dressing the doll. The wig can be glued back on once the doll is dressed.

2 Turn the dress to the right side, catch the facing to the neck edge and press lightly. Use narrow bonding web to turn up the hems of the sleeves while the dress is still flat.

3 With right sides together, pin the side and underarm seams and stitch together, clipping the underarm seam to the sewing line. Turn the dress to the right side and try it on the doll. Use narrow bonding web to turn up the hem.

4 You will need three lengths of lace, each approximately 15 inches long before gathering (see page 67); you can use all white or introduce a contrasting color to match the pattern on the coat if you wish. One strip goes on the under side of the basic dress to represent a petticoat. The second strip, which may be colored if you wish, should be placed so that its lower edge is level with the bottom of the hem. The third strip should be placed just above the second.

5 Finish off the dress by sewing or gluing tiny pearl beads up the front. You can also decorate it with a rose and a lace trim around the neckline if you wish.

~ MAKING THE LACE FRILLS ~

Using the two widths of lace gives the frill extra body. If you prefer, however, you could use ordinary edging lace, ¾ inch wide, gathered by hand or on a machine. Although the lace can be sewn by hand, it is quicker and neater to use a machine.

1 Lay the edging lace on the insertion lace and stitch the whole length together with a medium stitch. Cut to the required length (see instructions). Using the longest stitch on your sewing machine, sew three rows. The first row is at the top edge of the lace; the second row should be just above the line of stitching joining the three lengths of lace; and the third row should be at the lower edge of the lace. Use a contrasting color for the second and third rows.

2 Pull the threads up as tightly as you can. Press the gathered lace under a damp cloth and allow to cool. Carefully remove the colored gathering threads and ease out to the required length, taking great care not to break the remaining stitches. When the lace frill is the correct length, machine with a medium stitch across the first row of stitches or catch by hand.

~ MAKING A ROSE ~

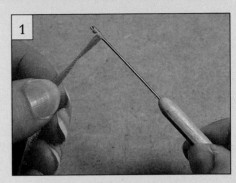

YOU WILL NEED

- A fine quilling stick
- 1 yard silk ribbon, ⅛ inch wide
- Clear all-purpose adhesive
- Scissors
- Needle
- Sewing thread

1 Slide the end of the ribbon between the teeth of the rose making tool and hold it in place with a tiny spot of adhesive. Twist the handle of the rose maker to the right and, at the same time, twist the ribbon in the other direction with your other hand, holding it in position with a spot of adhesive.

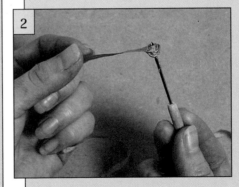

2 Continue to turn the tool and twist the ribbon, adding tiny spots of adhesive after each turn, until the rose measures the required size.

3 Glue the last turn well. Slide the rose carefully off the tool, cut the ribbon neatly, turning and gluing the end under, and stitch it through the center to a dress or hat. These roses are usually flat enough to be glued in place if you prefer.

~ MAKING A BOW ~

YOU WILL NEED

- Wooden cotton reel or piece of wood 2 inches long
- Hammer
- 2 small nails
- Metal file
- 1 yard silk ribbon, ⅛ inch wide
- Forceps or tweezers
- Scissors

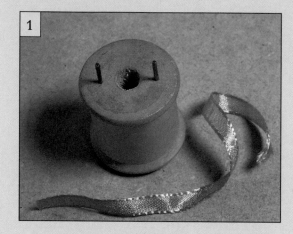

1 Hammer two small nails into the top of an old wooden cotton reel or a suitably sized piece of wood. Smooth the heads of the nails with a file.

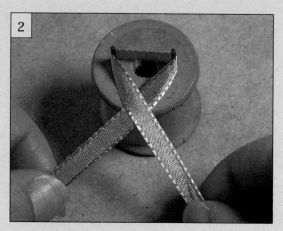

2 Place the ribbon around the nails. Bring the ends to the front and cross the left over the right.

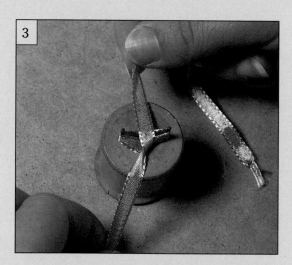

3 Take the end of the lower piece of ribbon over to the back.

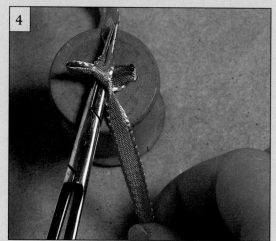

4 Use forceps or tweezers to bring it back to the front under the ribbon wrapped around the nails and under the end held at the front.

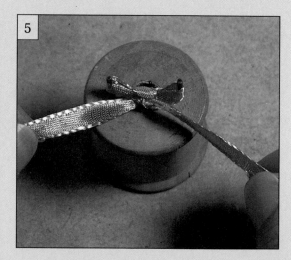

5 Tie the two ends at the front firmly together, slide the ribbon off the nails and trim the ribbons level with the bow.

MAKING THE COAT

1 Cut out two coat pieces, one a lining. With right sides together, stitch around from one hem edge, right round to the other hem edge. Clip the neck and the underarm edges to the sewing line.

2 Turn the coat through to the right side. Use a needle or pin to pull the seam out. Press lightly.

3 Try the coat on the doll, placing it, with the lining outwards, over the shoulders. Hem the back so that it is level with the front. Pin, then catch by hand the side seams.

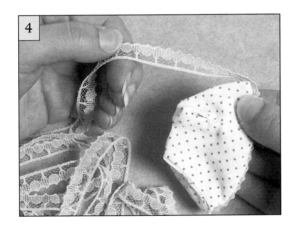

4 Turn the coat the right way out. Stitch edging lace around the inside of the front edge, then stitch matching or contrasting Picot trimmings along the top edge if you wish.

5 Make a bonnet with a lace frill (as for the dress). Pull up the gathers tightly and sew the back edge together, covering the back with a small embroidered motif or a small motif cut off a length of piqué. Add ribbons and bows to each side and fasten a small length of shirring elastic to run under the chin and hold the bonnet in place.

9

SAILOR BOY

~

BOYS WERE OFTEN DRESSED IN SAILOR
UNIFORMS IN LATE VICTORIAN AND EDWARDIAN
TIMES. THIS UNIFORM, WHICH WILL FIT A DOLL
ABOUT 4 INCHES TALL, IS MADE FROM FIVE
PATTERN PIECES.

YOU WILL NEED

- Tracing paper
- Pencil
- Pins
- Scissors
- Needle
- Sewing thread
- Narrow bonding web
- All-purpose adhesive
- Forceps or tweezers
- Sewing machine (optional)

FOR THE PANTS

- 6 inches white cotton fabric

FOR THE SHIRT

- 8 inches white cotton fabric
- Red felt pen
- 3 inches navy blue ribbon, ⅛ inch wide
- 6 inches navy blue cotton fabric
- 6 inches iron-on backing fabric (such as Vilene)

FOR THE HAT

- 3 inches white cotton fabric
- 3 inches navy blue ribbon, ⅛ inch wide

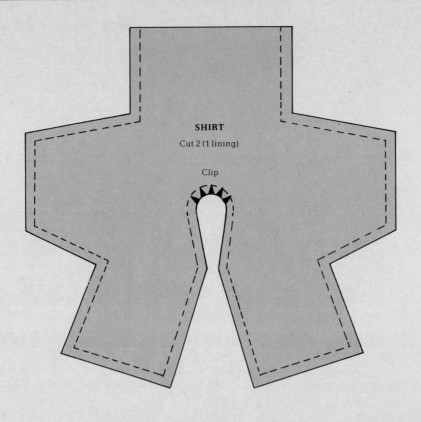

SHIRT

Cut 2 (1 lining)

Clip

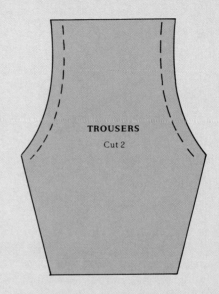

TROUSERS

Cut 2

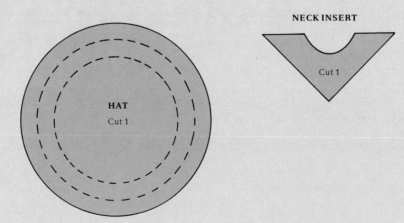

HAT

Cut 1

NECK INSERT

Cut 1

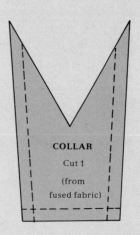

COLLAR

Cut 1

(from fused fabric)

MAKING
THE
PANTS

1 Cut out two pant pieces from white cotton fabric and stitch the front center seam, leaving a ¼ inch seam allowance. Use bonding web to turn up the hems at the bottom of the legs and around the waist.

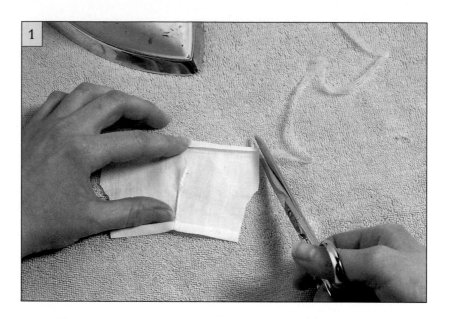

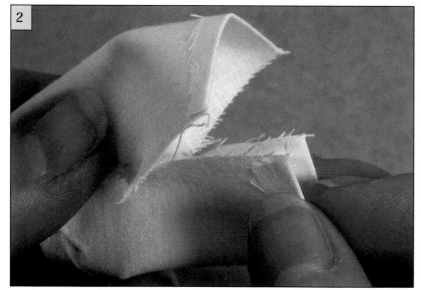

2 Turn the right sides together and stitch the center back seam. Refold, matching front and back seams.

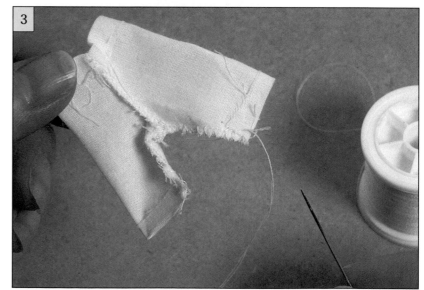

3 Stitch the crotch and inner leg seams. Turn the pants the right way out. Press them and place them on the doll, catching them with tiny stitches around the doll's waist.

MAKING — THE — SHIRT

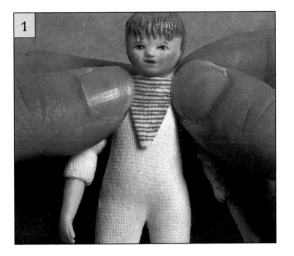

1 Cut out a V-shaped piece of white fabric for the dickey and rule fine red lines horizontally across it. Glue it to the doll's body around the neck.

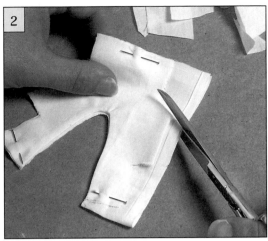

2 Cut out two shirt pieces, one as a lining. Pin them together and stitch them up the back seam around the arms, up the front, around the neck and back down to the back hem. Leave the back hem open. Clip the neck to the stitching line.

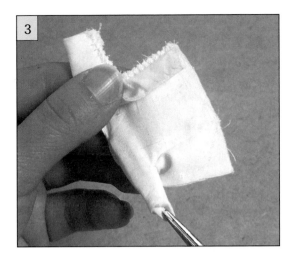

3 Turn the shirt through to the right sides, using forceps or tweezers to turn the sleeves through and to neaten the seams. Press lightly. Hem the back so that it is level with the front, turning up the outside and slip stitching it to the lining. Put the shirt on the doll, lining outwards, pinning it in place at the front and pinning the underarm and side seams to fit. Remove the pins at the front and slip stitch the underarm and side seams, beginning at the cuff.

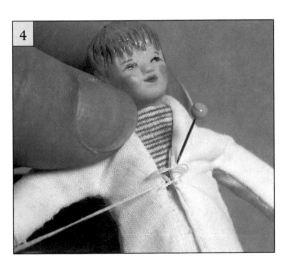

4 Turn the shirt to the right side and put it on the doll, pinning it in position so that the red-striped dickey can be seen. Catch the shirt in position down the front and use tiny stitches to attach it to the pants.

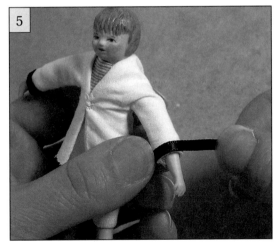

5 Glue navy blue ribbon around the cuffs of the shirt.

6

Fold the navy blue cotton fabric in two and place a piece of bonding material between the pieces. Press as directed to fuse the two pieces together. Cut the collar out of this piece. Use the smallest possible stitch and white cotton to sew a line ⅛ inch from the edge all round. Place the collar on the doll, sewing the points together and fixing them at the lower end of the V-shaped neck. If the collar will not lie flat at the back, hold it in place with one or two spots of adhesive.

7

Use narrow navy blue ribbon to make a bow (see page 68) and glue it to the bottom of the collar.

MAKING
— THE —
H A T

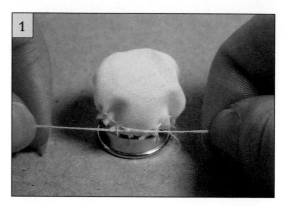

1

Cut out a circle of white cotton fabric and make two parallel rows of tiny running stitches around the circumference. Place an ordinary sewing thimble on the table in front of you as a guide and gather the circle over it, pulling it about three-quarters of the way down.

2

Run adhesive around the bottom edge of the fabric and attach a piece of navy blue ribbon. When the adhesive is dry remove the hat from the thimble and trim off any white threads that can be seen.

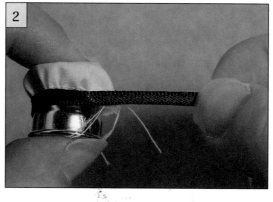

3

Put the hat on the doll's head, flattening the top so that it looks like a sailor's cap.

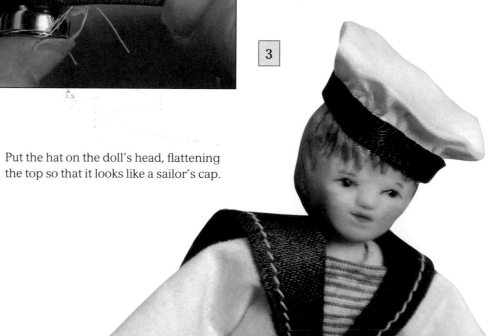

10

VICTORIAN MAID

~

NO VICTORIAN HOUSEHOLD WOULD BE
COMPLETE WITHOUT AT LEAST ONE MAID. MOST
OF THESE DOLLS ARE DRESSED IN STRIPED
MATERIAL, AND THE "ONE-WAY" PATTERN OF THIS
FABRIC MEANS THAT THE DRESS IS MADE WITH
SHOULDER SEAMS, ALTHOUGH THE LINING IS IN
ONE PIECE. APRONS AND CAPS USUALLY
IDENTIFIED JUST WHERE THE MAIDS WERE
WORKING. THIS MAID WOULD BE EQUALLY AT
HOME HELPING THE COOK OR DOING THE
CLEANING.

YOU WILL NEED

- Tracing paper
- Pencil
- Pins
- Scissors
- Needle
- Sewing thread
- Narrow bonding web
- Forceps or tweezers
- Sewing machine (optional)

FOR THE DRESS

- 9 inches striped cotton fabric
- 9 inches white cotton lining fabric
- 9 inches white bias binding
- All-purpose adhesive (optional)
- 9 inches white edging lace, 1 inch wide
- 6 hooks (optional)

FOR THE APRON

- 12 inches soft white cotton fabric
- 12 inches narrow tape

FOR THE CAP

- 6 inches white ribbon, ¼ inch wide

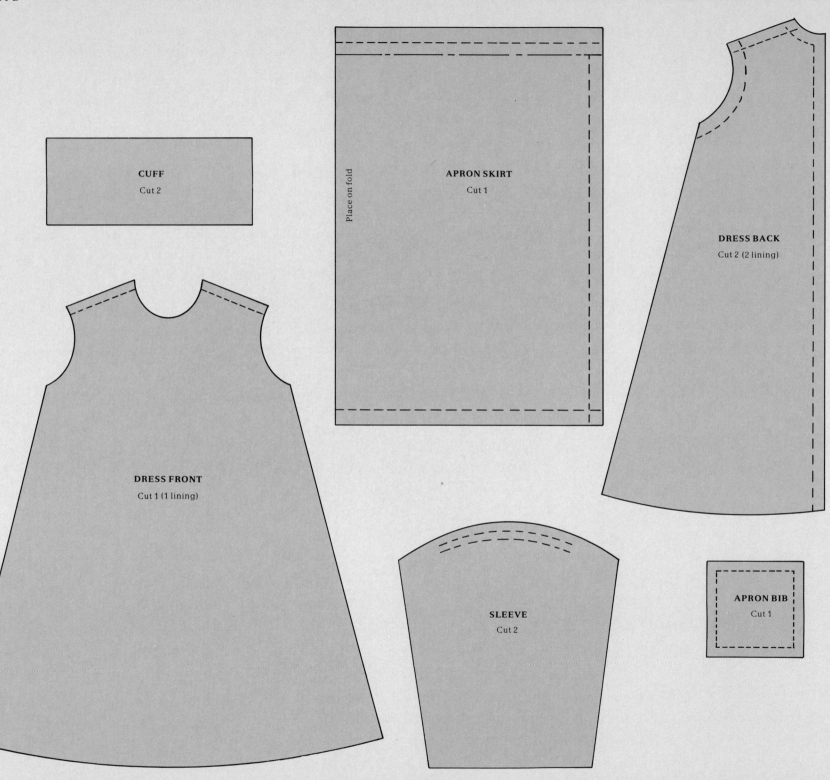

CUFF
Cut 2

APRON SKIRT
Cut 1

Place on fold

DRESS BACK
Cut 2 (2 lining)

DRESS FRONT
Cut 1 (1 lining)

SLEEVE
Cut 2

APRON BIB
Cut 1

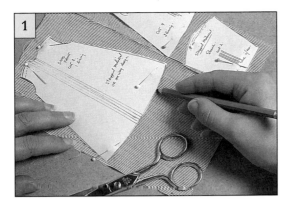

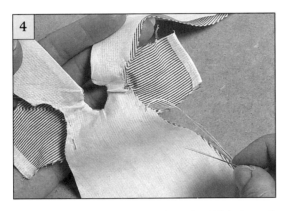

1 Cut out the front and two back pieces of the dress in the striped material only at this stage. Make sure that the stripes are straight. With right sides together, stitch the right and left shoulder seams together. Press lightly to open the seams.

2 Lay the striped material on top of the white lining fabric, pin in position and stitch up one side of the center back opening, around the neck and down the other center back opening.

3 Cut around the striped material, remove the pins, clip around the neck seam and turn to the right side. Try on the doll to check the fit around the neck. Also check the length and turn up the hem, stitching the striped fabric to the lining with slip stitch.

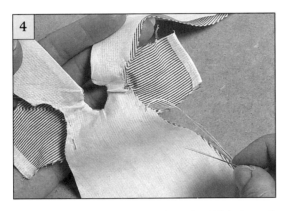

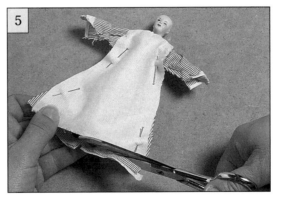

4 Cut two sleeve pieces in striped fabric and two cuff pieces from white lining fabric. Stitch a cuff to the wrist end of each sleeve piece and turn up, leaving about ⅛ inch showing on the right side. Use bonding web to hold the cuff in position. Stitch two parallel rows of tiny running stitches across the top of the sleeve pieces and gather them slightly. With right sides together, stitch the sleeves to the dress front and back, sewing through both striped and lining fabrics and easing the fullness to the top. Clip the fabric to the stitching line.

5 With the lining outwards, try the dress on the doll. Pin the back seam, then pin the side and underarm seams to fit. Remove the pins from the back, take off the dress and stitch the side and underarm seams, beginning at the cuff and stitching down to the hem at each side. If you are using a sewing machine, use a small zigzag stitch for extra strength. Hem the dress by stitching white bias binding, right sides

together, around the raw edge. Turn the binding in and catch by hand or adhesive to the dress. Trim the edge of the lining with lace, either stitched or glued in position. Finish off the neck edge with white bias binding. Place the dress on the doll and either oversew the back seam or, if you think you may want to redress the doll at some stage, fasten it with small hooks and thread loops.

MAKING
— THE —
APRON

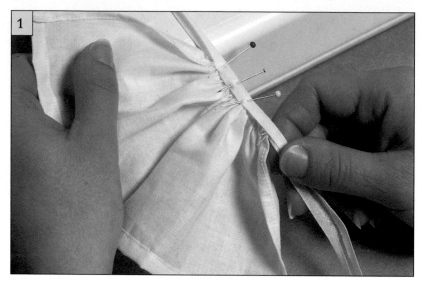

1. Cut out the skirt of the apron from the white cotton fabric, remembering to place the template on the fold of the fabric. Hem the side edges. The maid's dress should be about 1cm/½in longer than the apron, so check the length before turning up the bottom hem. Use bonding web or stitch by hand. Stitch two parallel rows of running stitches along the top edge of the apron and gather the fullness carefully; the apron should completely cover the doll's skirt. Pin white bias binding along the top edge with right sides together and stitch over the apron gathers. Oversew the loose ends of the bias binding to form the apron ties.

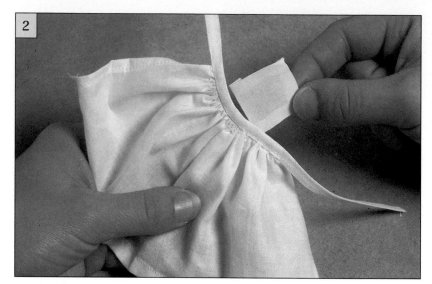

2. Cut out the apron bib. Turn in 5mm/¼in hem on all sides. Pin the bib in place in the centre of the apron and check again to fit.

3. Tie the apron in a bow at the back and glue or catch by hand the top of the bib to the dress front. If you wish, make a small cap with white ribbon.

11

EDWARDIAN
MAID

~

THE TASKS OF MAIDS IN EDWARDIAN TIMES
COULD ALSO BE IDENTIFIED BY THEIR CLOTHES.
THE MAIDS WHO WAITED AT MEAL TIMES WERE
DRESSED MORE ELEGANTLY THAN, FOR EXAMPLE,
THOSE WHO WORKED UNDER THE COOK IN THE
KITCHEN. THIS MAID, IN HER BLACK DRESS,
ORGANDIE APRON WITH LACE TRIM AND LACE-
EDGED COLLAR AND CAP, IS CLEARLY ONE OF THE
MAIDS WHO WAS SEEN "ABOVE STAIRS".

YOU WILL NEED

- Tracing paper
- Pencil
- Pins
- Scissors
- Needle
- Sewing thread
- Narrow bonding web
- Forceps or tweezers
- All-purpose adhesive
- Sewing machine (optional)

FOR THE PANTALOONS

- 6 inches white cotton lawn
- 6 inches white edging lace, ¼ inch wide
- Shirring elastic (optional)

FOR THE DRESS

- 12 inches black cotton fabric
- 6 inches white edging lace, ½ inch wide
- 12 inches white cotton lining fabric
- 12 inches white bias binding
- 18 inches white edging lace, 1 inch wide
- 2 inches white organdie
- White craft paint
- 6 inches fine white Picot trim

FOR THE APRON

- 6 inches white organdie
- 12 inches white edging lace, ¼ inch wide
- 12 inches white bias binding

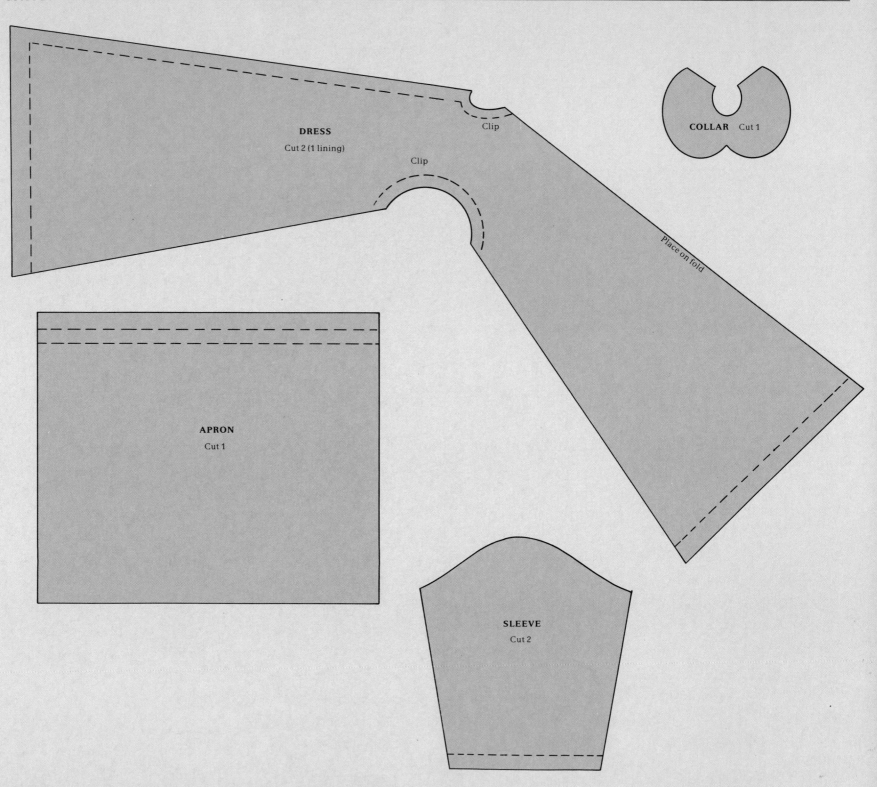

DRESS
Cut 2 (1 lining)

Clip

Clip

Place on fold

COLLAR Cut 1

APRON
Cut 1

SLEEVE
Cut 2

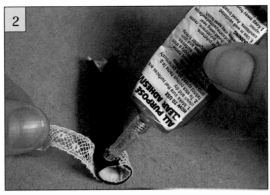

MAKING — THE — DRESS

1 Before you begin the dress, make the pantaloons as for the Victorian lady (see page 42). Cut out two sleeve pieces in black fabric. Turn up the hems with bonding web and stitch the underarm seams. Use forceps or tweezers to turn the sleeves to the right sides.

2 Glue cuffs of narrow edging lace around the bottom edges of the sleeves.

3 Place the sleeves on the doll's arms and catch them in place at the shoulder with a few small stitches.

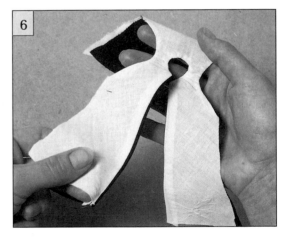

4 Cut out two dress pieces, one in black cotton and one for the lining, remembering to place the dress front against a fold in the fabric.

5 Pin the right sides together and stitch around the underarm seams and up the two center back seams and around the neck. Clip to the stitching line and press lightly.

6 Turn to the right side, using forceps or tweezers if necessary so that the seams lie flat. Press again.

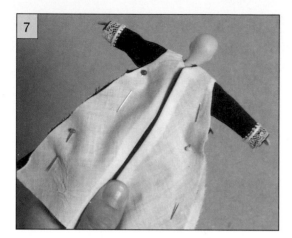

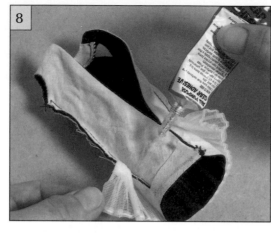

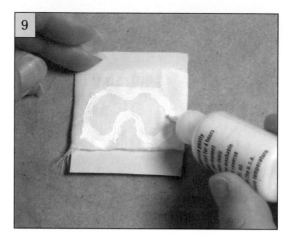

7 Put the dress on the doll with the lining outwards. Pin the back seam together, then pin the side seams to fit. Unpin the back and stitch the side seams.

8 Use white bias binding to hem the dress. Stitch the binding, right sides together, to the black dress, turn it up and glue or stitch it to the lining. Glue or stitch gathered edging lace to the lining. This represents the petticoat.

9 Place a small piece of white organdie over the outline of the collar and trace around the edge with white craft paint.

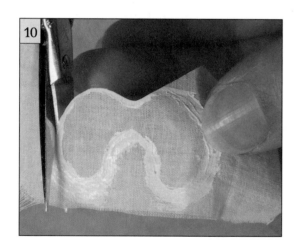

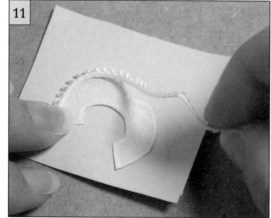

10 Allow the paint to dry and cut out the collar. The paint will help prevent the organdie from fraying.

11 Glue the Picot edging around the edge of the collar.

12 Put the dress on the doll, oversew the center back seam. Catch the shoulder to the sleeves with tiny stitches. Glue the collar in position.

MAKING THE APRON

1 Cut out the apron from white organdie and hand stitch white edging lace around three sides.

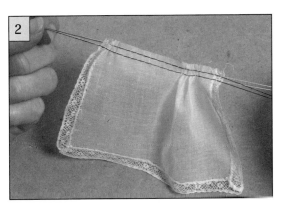

2 Use a sewing machine to stitch two parallel lines of large stitches along the top edge. Use a different color thread on the bobbin. Fold in two to find the center and mark it with a pin. Find the center of a length of bias binding 1½ inches long and mark it with a pin. Pull up the gathers and stitch the bias binding, right sides together and with pins aligned, along the top edge. Remove the colored gathering threads, and oversew the bias binding at the back.

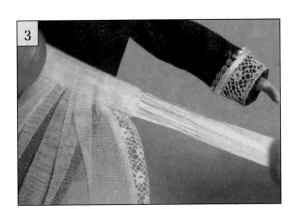

3 Cut the remaining length of bias binding in two. Fasten each piece to the waistband of the apron and tie in a bow at the back of the doll.

4 Finish off the doll by wrapping a piece of ¼ inch edging lace around the bun of the wig.

~ MAKING AN EDWARDIAN-STYLE WIG ~

To finish off the Edwardian maid, you might want to give her a period wig, around which the little lace cap can be fitted.

YOU WILL NEED

- 6 inches mohair
- Scissors
- Needle
- Sewing thread to match mohair
- Plastic film
- Rubber band
- Clear adhesive

Cut two lengths of mohair, each 3 inches long. Gently brush the mohair, holding it down with one hand. Keep any loose hairs to one side. Place the two lengths of mohair side by side and tease out until they match the measurement around the doll's head. Using the smallest possible stitches, sew a line ¼ inch from one edge.

Cover the doll's head with a small piece of plastic film, holding it in position with a rubber band around the doll's neck. Put a thin layer of adhesive over the hair area of the plastic film, taking care to keep it within what will be the doll's hairline.

Place the stitched line along the front hairline and press down well. Use any combings or spare pieces of hair to pad the hair on top of the head, then smooth the hair back over the head, pulling the long ends back and to the top of the doll's head. Catch the hair in place with a thread. Turn in any loose long ends to make a bun. Remove the rubber band and peel off the plastic film with the mohair attached. Cut off the spare plastic film. Trim the plastic film neatly to the hairline. Cover the head with a thin layer of adhesive and place the wig on the head, folding any visible pieces of plastic film neatly under the wig.

12

COOK

~

IN MOST VICTORIAN AND EDWARDIAN
HOUSEHOLDS THE COOK WAS, AFTER THE
BUTLER, THE MOST IMPORTANT OF THE BELOW
STAIRS SERVANTS. HER DRESS WAS DIFFERENT
FROM THAT WORN BY THE MAIDS, AND HER
APRON AND CAP WERE ADDITIONAL SYMBOLS OF
AUTHORITY. THIS IS A SIMPLE PATTERN TO MAKE
AND ONE THAT CAN BE EASILY ADAPTED FOR
OTHER PURPOSES – FOR EXAMPLE, LEFT OPEN AT
THE FRONT, IT COULD BE USED AS A COAT OR IT
COULD BE SHORTENED AND USED AS A JACKET.

YOU WILL NEED

- Tracing paper
- Pencil
- Pins
- Scissors
- Needle
- Sewing thread
- Narrow bonding web
- Forceps or tweezers
- All-purpose adhesive
- Sewing machine (optional)

FOR THE PANTALOONS

- 6 inches white cotton lawn
- 6 inches white edging lace, ¼ inch wide
- Shirring elastic (optional)

FOR THE DRESS

- 9 inches blue cotton fabric
- 9 inches white cotton lining fabric
- 12 inches white bias binding
- 12 inches gathered white edging lace, 1 inch wide

FOR THE APRON

- 12 inches white cotton fabric
- 12 inches white bias binding

FOR THE CAP

- 2½ × 1½ inch piece of white cotton fabric
- Embroidered motif or motif from Picot edging
- 2 inches white ribbon, ⅛ inch wide

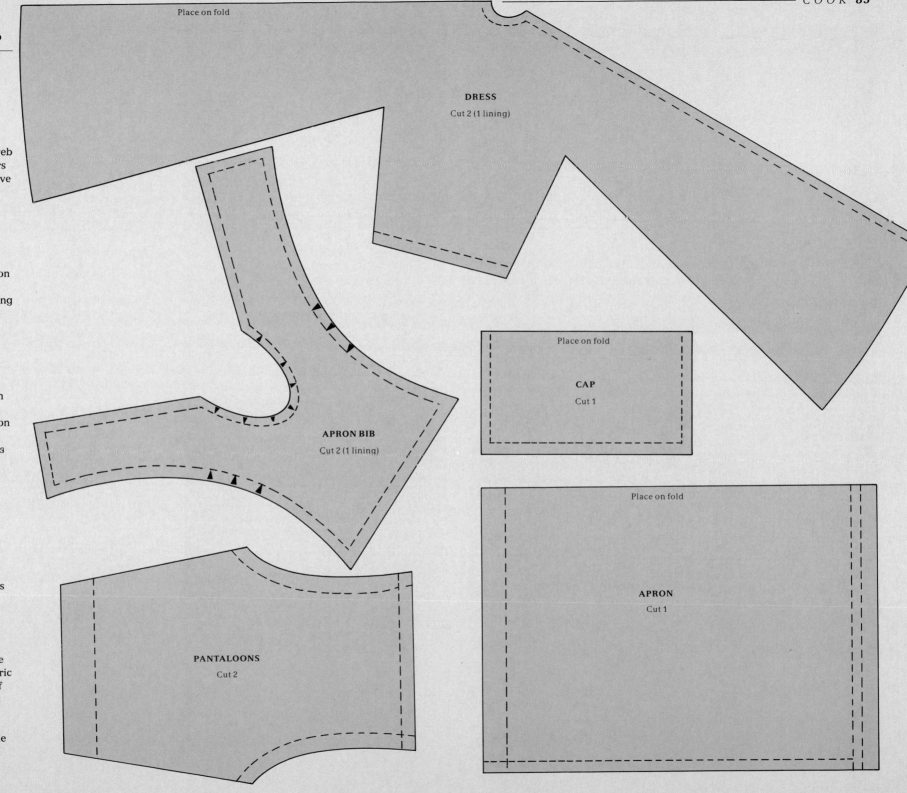

Place on fold

DRESS
Cut 2 (1 lining)

APRON BIB
Cut 2 (1 lining)

Place on fold

CAP
Cut 1

PANTALOONS
Cut 2

Place on fold

APRON
Cut 1

MAKING THE DRESS

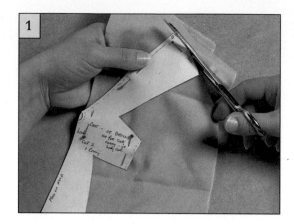

1 Before you make the dress, make the pantaloons, following the instructions for the Victorian Lady on page 42. Cut two dress pieces, one in blue and one in white lining fabric, remembering to place the center front against a fold.

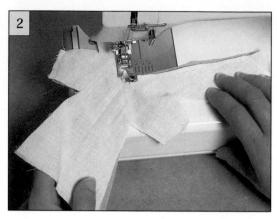

2 Pin the dress and lining pieces together with right sides facing. Stitch up one back edge, around the neck and down the other back edge. Stitch across the bottom of the sleeves. Clip the neck to the stitch line.

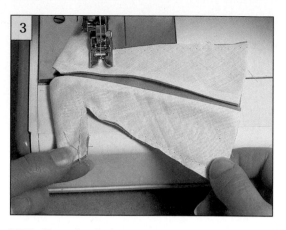

3 Turn the dress to the right side, using tweezers or forceps to neaten the seam edges. Press lightly. With the lining facing outwards, put the dress on the doll, pin the back opening together and pin the underarm and side seams together. Unpin the back and stitch the underarm and side seams, starting at the cuff edge. Turn the dress to the right side and turn back about ¼ inch of the sleeves so that the white shows as a cuff. Catch down with a few tiny stitches.

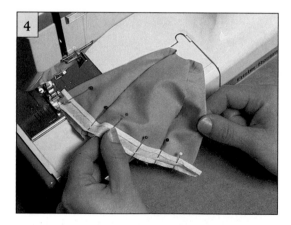

4 With right sides facing, stitch bias binding along the hem of the blue dress. Turn up the binding and glue or slip stitch it to the lining.

5 Stitch or glue a layer of gathered lace around the bottom of the lining as a "petticoat".

6 With right sides facing, stitch a short piece of white bias binding around the neck edge as a collar. Turn under and glue or slip stitch to the lining. Put the dress on the doll and slip stitch or oversew the back seam.

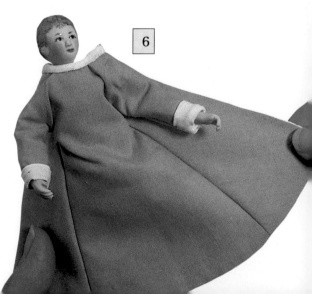

MAKING
— THE —
APRON

1 Cut out the skirt of the apron, remembering to place one edge of the template against a fold in the fabric. Cut out two apron bibs.

2 Turn up a hem at the bottom edge of ¼ inch and hems at the two short edges of ⅛ inch. Stitch by hand or by machine two parallel rows of stitches along the top edge and gather to fit bib. If you use a sewing machine, use the longest stitch for the gathering stitches.

~ MAKING THE CAP ~

1 Use the template to cut a piece of white fabric. Fold it in half and stitch the sides. Turn to the right side, neaten the seam edges and press. Gather the open edge with two rows of small running stitches, pulling the fabric up as tightly as possible. Cover this with a small embroidered motif.

2 Turn back the front ⅛ inch and add two ribbon ties. Place the cap on the doll's head and tie the ribbon neatly under the chin to hold the cap on.

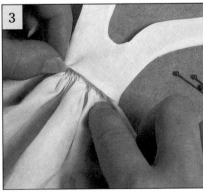

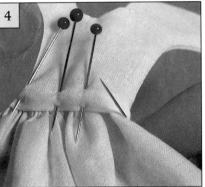

3 Stitch the two bib pieces together by sewing all around the sides and neck opening, but leaving the waist seam open. Use forceps or tweezers to turn the bib to the right side and to neaten the seams. Press lightly. Turn up the hem of the bib and insert the gathered apron skirt in the bottom of the bib, checking for fit.

4 Pin the gathered apron skirt in position between the front and lining of the bib. Stitch neatly in position from both front and back.

5 Neatly oversew the bias binding, cut it in half and attach one piece to each side of the waist of the apron. Put the apron on the doll, tying it in a bow at the back. Cross the long ends of the bib over at the back of the doll and stitch them to the apron ties.

~ BUTCHER ~

Throughout the history of fashion, some styles of clothing appear to have been worn by different trades and professions. The English butcher, for example, has been described, illustrated and photographed wearing clothes that seem hardly to have changed for over a century. This butcher might be at home in a high street butcher's store today, but he is equally appropriately dressed for the late Victorian or early Edwardian times. His pants can be made of any dark material, and his shirt is gathered above the elbow with elastic, a style that could be used to dress, say, a butler. The striped apron is, however, typical of a butcher. Make the pants and shirt according to the instructions for the Victorian Man (see page 51) but use the sleeve template shown here. Use shirring elastic to hold the fullness of the shirt above the elbow.

YOU WILL NEED

- Tracing paper
- Pencil
- Pins
- Scissors
- 4 × 4 inches blue striped cotton fabric
- All-purpose adhesive
- Narrow bonding web
- 12 inches dark blue ribbon, ⅛ inch wide

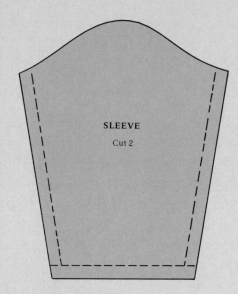

SLEEVE

Cut 2

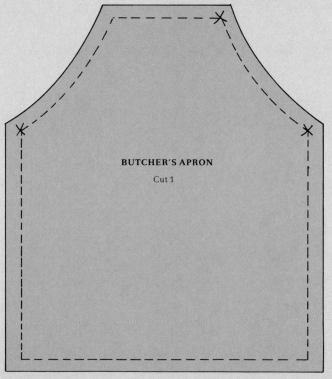

BUTCHER'S APRON

Cut 1

1   Use the template to cut out the shape of the apron.

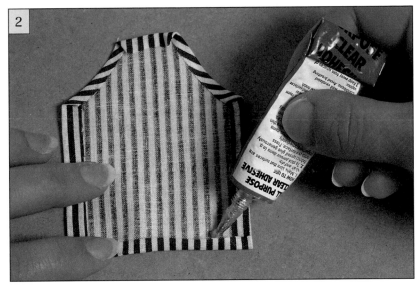

2   Glue or use bonding web to turn in the ¼ inch hem all round.

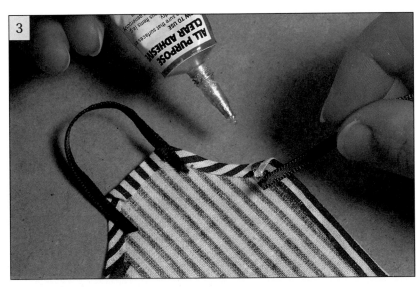

3   Glue the ties for the waist and to go around the neck. You might find it easier to glue just one end of the neck ribbon before you dress the doll, finishing the other end when the apron is in place.

4   Place the apron on the doll and tie it neatly at the back.

13

PILOT

~

ONE OF THE MOST DELIGHTFUL ASPECTS OF
EDWARDIAN LIFE WAS THE HABIT OF WEARING
EXACTLY THE RIGHT OUTFIT FOR EVERY ACTIVITY
OR SOCIAL EVENT. THIS WAS PARTICULARLY
NOTICEABLE IN SOME OF THE MORE DARING
SPORTING EVENTS SUCH AS THE NEW PASSION
FOR DRIVING MOTOR CARS AND FOR FLYING. OUR
PILOT, FROM HIS HELMET AND GOGGLES DOWN
TO HIS LEATHER BOOTS, WOULD HAVE BEEN IN
THE HEIGHT OF FASHION. JODHPURS AND A
LEATHER, BLOUSON-STYLE JACKET WERE *DE
RIGUEUR*, AND EVERY PILOT HAD A SCARF AND
GOGGLES. A PARACHUTE WAS NOT, HOWEVER,
PART OF HIS KIT.

YOU WILL NEED

- Tracing paper
- Pencil
- Pins
- Scissors
- Narrow bonding web
- Needle
- Sewing thread
- Forceps or tweezers
- All-purpose adhesive
- Sewing machine (optional)
- Leather needle
- Fine or black ballpoint pen

FOR THE SHIRT

- 12 inches white cotton fabric
- 6 inches brown ribbon, ⅛ inch wide
- 3 inches shirring elastic

FOR THE JODHPURS

- 9 inches khaki-colored fine tweed fabric

FOR THE BOOTS

- 4 × 1½ inches soft brown glove leather
- 4 small bulldog clips
- Black shirring elastic
- Small pieces of black leather for soles

FOR THE JACKET

- 12 inches soft brown glove leather

FOR THE HELMET, GOGGLES AND SCARF

- Plastic film
- Rubber bands
- 1 tbsp PVA
- 2 tbsp hot water
- 3 × 3 inches buckram
- 3 × 3 inches soft dark brown or black glove leather
- Small piece of pale brown or yellow glove leather
- Leather punch with large hole
- Clear plastic
- Ballpoint pen
- 3 × ¼ inch white silk

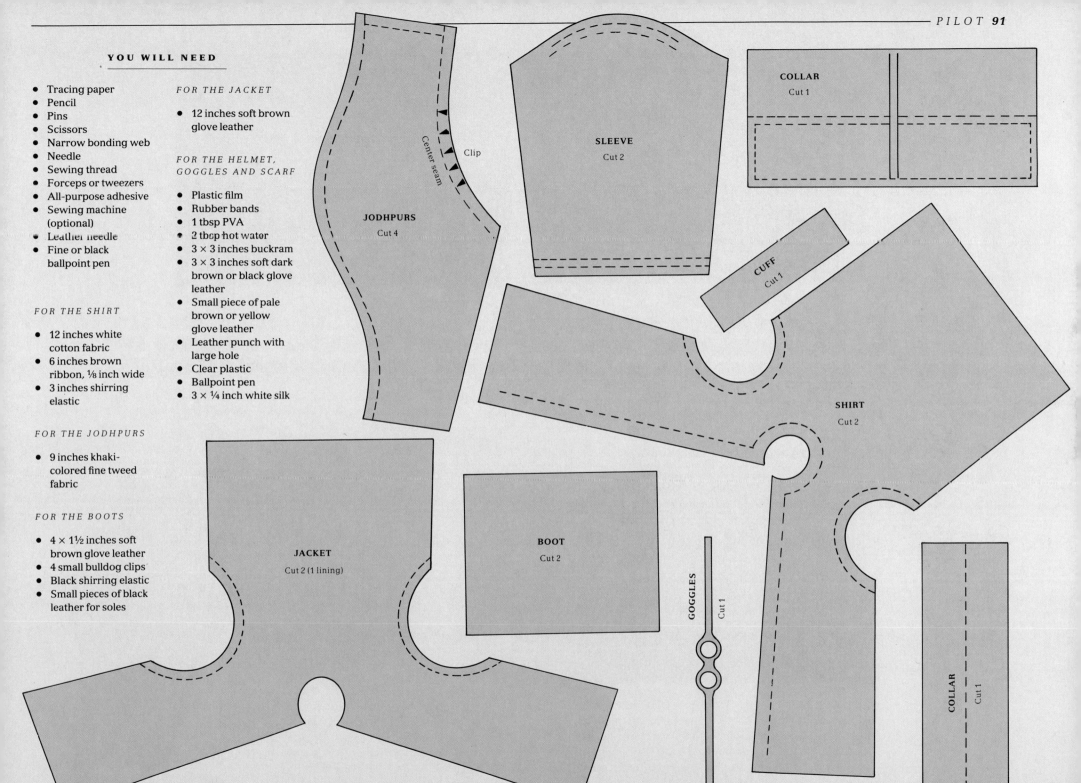

MAKING THE SHIRT

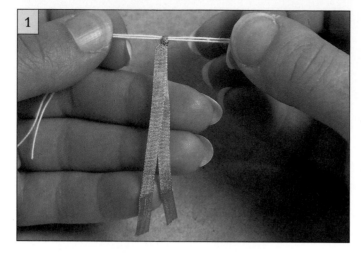

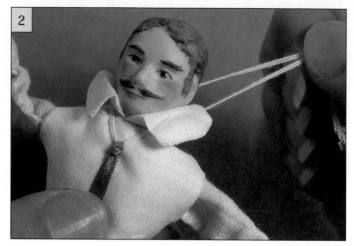

1 Make a sleeveless shirt, using the template for the front and back of the shirt and collar given here, according to the instructions for the Victorian Man (see page 51). Put the shirt on the doll. Fold the brown ribbon over the elastic and stitch it down to resemble a knot in a tie.

2 Fasten the elastic at the back of the neck under the collar.

MAKING THE JODHPURS

1 Cut out four pieces. Stitch the side seams and use bonding web to turn in the hems at the waist and ankle. With right sides together, stitch the center back seam. Refold the right sides together and stitch the inside leg seams.

2 Clip the center seams, turn to the right side and press lightly. Put the jodhpurs on the doll, tucking the shirt into the waistband, and stitch neatly to the shirt.

MAKING
THE
BOOTS

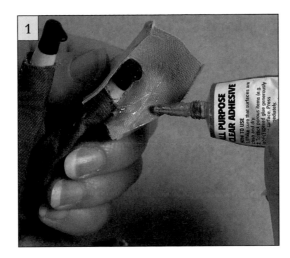

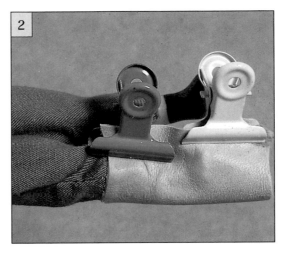

1 Use the template to cut out two pieces of glove leather. These pieces cover the bottom of the jodhpurs and are wrapped around the leg.

2 Glue the leather in position and hold it tightly at the front of the doll's leg with small bulldog clips. Allow the glue to dry.

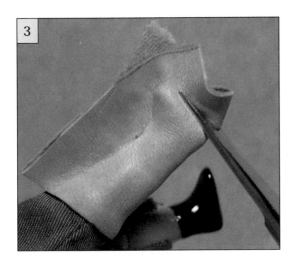

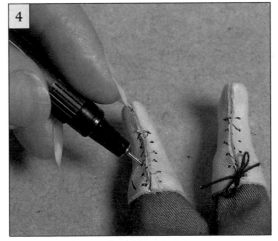

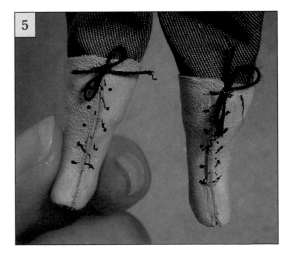

3 Use very sharp scissors to clip off the leather from around the toes and up the front of the leg. Make sure that the line up the front of the leg where the two pieces of leather meet is particularly neatly cut.

4 Use a black ballpoint pen to mark buttons and laces on the front of the boots. Use a leather needle to thread a length of black shirring elastic through the top of the holes and tie the elastic in a bow. Trim off the ends.

5 Trim under the soles, close to the porcelain foot, and glue small pieces of black leather under the feet to represent the soles of the boots.

MAKING
— THE —
JACKET

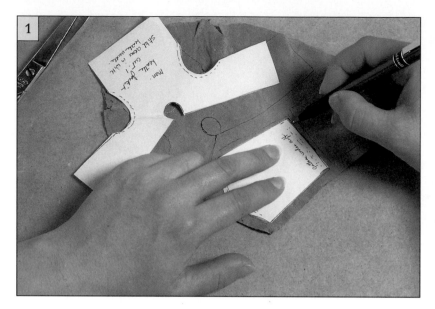

1 Cut out one jacket piece, two sleeves, one collar and two cuffs, using the smooth side of the leather as the right side.

2 Use a leather needle to sew the sleeves to the jacket body. Fold the cuffs in half and glue them to the bottom of the sleeves. Oversew the underarm and side seams.

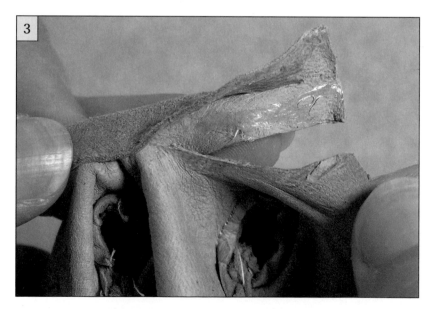

3 Fold the collar in two and glue it in position around the outside of the neck.

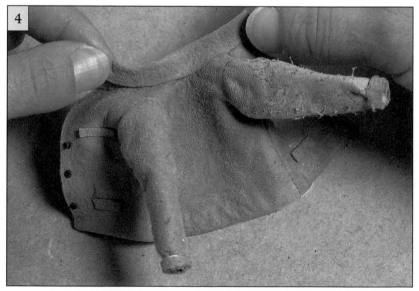

4 Turn over the collar and glue it firmly to the neckline. Glue on little offcuts of leather to represent pocket flaps.

MAKING THE HELMET, GOGGLES AND SCARF

1 Cover the doll's head with plastic film, holding it firmly around the neck with rubber bands.

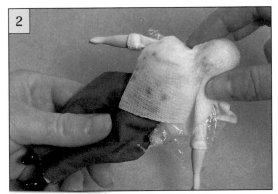

2 Mix the PVA and hot water in a bowl and soak the buckram and leather for at least 30 seconds. Place the buckram over the doll's head and smooth it down as firmly as possible, holding it tightly in place with a rubber band.

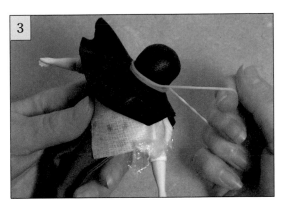

3 Smooth the soaked leather over the buckram, using a rubber band to hold it over the doll's head. Leave to dry completely.

4 Cut out the goggles, using a leather punch to cut out the eye holes. Glue circles of clear plastic behind the eye holes if you wish.

5 Cut off the rubber bands and slide the shaped material off the head. Remove the plastic film. Use a ballpoint pen to mark the outline of the helmet, remembering that it should come well down over the forehead and that there should be earflaps. Cut around the outline a little at a time. Glue the goggles in place.

6 Finish the pilot off with strips of dark leather as a belt and strap over the right shoulder, glued in place. Tie the scarf around his neck.

~ GLOSSARY ~

Bisque Also sometimes known as biscuit ware, bisque is a kiln-fired material used for making doll parts, especially heads, lower arms and lower legs.

Casting This is the process of making hollow-ware by casting slip (liquid clay) in a mold of plaster of Paris.

Cones Small shapes that soften and bend at predetermined temperatures. They are a reliable way of controlling and recording the point at which firing is complete.

Flash lines or flashing These are the lines caused by the joins in a mold that may be seen on the article when it is removed from the mold.

Fettling Flash lines on greenware may be removed by fettling, which is done with tools and a brush.

Greenware The dry but unfired cast doll parts are known as greenware when they are first removed from the mold.

Incise Parts of a doll may be marked – with the date or some means of identifying the maker – by incising a mark in soft clay.

Kiln-setter This name is given to types of kiln in which the temperature is controlled by a special cone.

Leather-hard Clay that has started to dry but that is still workable is described as leather-hard; at this stage it is still possible to change details on faces and hands, for example.

Pyrometer This instrument is used to measure kiln temperatures.

Thermocouple Some kilns are fitted with this control device, which turns off the electricity once the correct temperature has been reached.

Slip or casting slip Liquid clay.